FIXING YOUR CITY

Creating Thriving Neighborhoods and Adapting to a Changing World

PRAISE FOR CRANDALL ARAMBULA

Missoula, MT – "Crandall Arambula has repeatedly demonstrated why they are indeed one of the best urban planning firms in America."

Ellen Buchanan, Director
Missoula Redevelopment Agency

Aurora, CO – "They have a public involvement process that comes as close to perfect as one can expect."

Loretta Daniel, Former Principal
Planner, City of Aurora, Colorado

Albany, OR – "Downtown Albany has been transformed because of Crandall's guidance. From the initial over-arching plan, to public participation, and implementation – our community is thriving!"

Kate Porsche, Former Economic Development
and Urban Renewal Director, Albany, Oregon

Lincoln, NE – "In the past 10 years a total of $1.3 billion of investment has occurred in downtown. I can confidently say this investment is in large part the result of the 2005 Downtown Master Plan Crandall Arambula envisioned for Lincoln."

Terry Uland, President,
Downtown Lincoln Association

Racine, WI – "Developers have time and again shared with us that the downtown plan, along with the implementation strategy, has given them confidence to invest in downtown Racine. Over $230 million of development has been announced since plan completion."

Devin Sutherland, Former Executive
Director, Downtown Racine Corporation

Whitefish, MT – "Every project identified during our downtown master planning process has had a positive economic effect, while preserving the historic character of the community. The experience and expertise of this firm is exceptional."

Rhonda Fitzgerald, Vice-Chair of
Heart of Whitefish Downtown Association

Edmonton, Alberta – "I worked with George and his excellent staff on numerous Transit Oriented Development (TOD) projects in Edmonton and Portland. Their work has always been fundamentally grounded, insightful and creative. They designed award-winning communities that were built."

Larry Ksionzyk, Former Principal
TOD Planner, Edmonton, Alberta

Knoxville, TN – "In leading Knoxville to a clear vision for its downtown, hundreds participated in the process and the final proposals were both visionary and realistic."

Marleen Davis, FAIA, Professor
& Former Dean of the University of
Tennessee College of Architecture

Bismarck, ND – "The Downtown Bismarck Subarea is still being referred to as the authoritative source in planning and implementation committees, both in public and private arenas."

Steve Saunders, Principal
Transportation Planner, Bismarck-Mandan
Metropolitan Planning Organization

Portland, OR – "I reviewed a presentation by George Crandall entitled *Portland Transformation Strategy.* I believe that this strategy will provide our city with innovative solutions for dealing with population growth, congestion, and global warming."

Ted Wheeler, Mayor of Portland, OR

FIXING YOUR CITY

*Creating Thriving
Neighborhoods
and Adapting to a
Changing World*

GEORGE CRANDALL

Fuller Press

Portland • Oregon

Publisher: Fuller Press | www.marilynsewell.com

Paperback ISBN-13 978-0-9961040-1-2 | ISBN-10 0-9961040-1-1
eBook ISBN-13 978-0-9961040-2-9 | ISBN-10 0-9961040-2-X

7 9 11 13 15 14 12 10 8

In Memoriam

Ann Crandall

Contents

Preface

The final essay in the book *Reconsidering Jane Jacobs,* by Thomas J. Campanella, identifies the legacies of the Jacobsian revolution and the factors that contributed to the decline of the planning profession.

As a planner in private practice for over forty years, I found Campanella's assessment to be accurate. I agree with the sad admission from members of his Chapel Hill planning faculty that our chosen field could be ranked as a "trivial profession."

Campanella identifies a fundamental problem in Jacobs's legacy that needs to be recognized and corrected. He writes:

> The literature on grassroots planning tends to assume a citizenry of Gandhian humanists. In fact, most people are not motivated by altruism but by self-interest . . . This is why it's a fool's errand to rely upon citizens to guide the planning process. Forget for a moment that most folks lack the knowledge to make intelligent decisions about the future of our cities. Most people are simply too busy, too apathetic, or too focused on their jobs or kids to be moved to action over issues unless those issues are at their doorstep. And once an issue is at their doorstep, fear sets on and reason flies out the window. So the very citizens least able to make objective decisions end up dominating the process, often wielding near-veto power over proposals.

Campanella concludes with comments about where the planning profession is today. Planners have become jacks-of-all-trades and masters of none. Parochial interests shape and guide the planning process. Neglecting broader societal interests, the planner's role has become that of "umpire or schoolyard monitor." The courage and vision that once distinguished the planning profession has become a rarity. The role of the planner has been reduced by planners themselves to small-ness and timidity.

Later in her life, Jacobs herself grew frustrated. In an April 1993 speech published in the *Ontario Planning Journal,* she stated, "Our offi-cial planning departments seem to be brain-dead in the sense that we cannot depend on them in any way, shape, or form for providing intel-lectual leadership in addressing urgent problems involving the physical future of the city."

The consequence of the Jacobsian legacy is the creation of plans that sit on the shelf. In every city where I am retained to produce a plan, I hear the same refrain: "We have been planning for years and nothing gets implemented. We don't want another shelf plan."

The problem is not public involvement per se. The problem is defective public involvement. *Fixing Your City* offers a practical, proven process for planning and public involvement that my firm has used suc-cessfully in dozens of towns and cities. Education and the presentation of viable options must inform public involvement. In my experience, an informed public will always make the right decisions.

It is my hope that the information in *Fixing Your City* will be helpful to the planning profession, enabling us to take our rightful place as professionals who can provide the leadership and direction that our ailing cities and country so badly need. In addition, my goal is to demystify the work of the profession and empower concerned citizens to become active participants in shaping their cities.

Introduction

Our cities can be fixed. They can flourish again.
And you can make a difference.

On a cool spring day, after a sixty-year absence, I drove into my hometown of Sudbury, Ontario. My wife wanted to see where my Canadian bush stories came from, and I wanted to see my parents' graves.

When I'd left Sudbury, the town had a population of 56,000 people. Now it was over 160,000. The barren black-rock landscape surrounding the city, created by acid rain from the smelting of ore early in the last century, was as I remembered it. But I wasn't prepared for the destruction of the once-vibrant city center.

The friendly downtown I remembered from my childhood was nowhere to be found. Missing were the grocery store where I would pick up what my mother needed for the evening meal; the two movie theaters where I would spend Saturday afternoons sitting in the first row; the toy store where I had my first job assembling bicycles for Christmas shoppers; the menswear store where I proudly purchased a red plaid vest; the jewelry store where I bought my first wristwatch with part of my summer earnings; and the record store where my friends and I would listen to the latest hits. Everything was gone.

The downtown now had drive-through banks, buildings with blank walls at the street level, and surface parking lots. The few remaining historic buildings were diminished by large-scale office buildings with characterless facades. To accommodate the automobiles flooding the city, curbside parking had been removed. I was stunned. What I remembered as an intimate downtown had turned into an unpleasant, pedestrian-hostile environment.

But that wasn't all. The safe, convenient walk from my old neighborhood to downtown was no longer possible. A chain-link fence blocked the way—erected to eliminate a railroad crossing that was once used by both cars and pedestrians. Now cars traveled downtown on a road without sidewalks, under the railroad tracks. A narrow 300-foot tunnel was built for pedestrians. Poorly lit, damp, with crude public art, it was accessed by steep stairs. A sign at the entry read: "WARNING! This underpass is monitored by electronic surveillance. Sudbury regional police service." It's not a place you would want to be on a dark night!

The downtown had lost its character. It was no longer a place to linger. It had become a place to drive through.

I had planned to spend a few days in Sudbury, visiting old haunts. Instead, I went to the cemetery, said my goodbyes, and left. I knew that I would never return. But even more importantly, I realized that my hometown was not unique. The tragedy is that "my town" exists everywhere.

This book provides practical advice about how to fix your city and help it thrive. It describes how change happens in cities and what you can do to become part of the process. It identifies what works and what doesn't in city transformation. It is not a book about city planning and urban theories. It is a go-to resource of innovative techniques that will guide you in responding to climate change and transforming your city, no matter what its size.

Fixing Your City: Creating Thriving Neighborhoods and Adapting to a Changing World was inspired by the public's frustration with the decline of its cities. As one citizen activist put it to me recently, "Why do cities get screwed up, become worse and worse, and nobody does anything about it?"

Fixing Your City answers that question and provides the information you need in order to become an effective advocate for change. By the time you finish this book, you will know that you, too, can make a difference. You will have the confidence to take effective action to make your city a more desirable place to live.

Wherever I travel across the United States, I hear the same concerns. Our downtown used to be a great place to visit and shop, residents say. Now it is a place to avoid. Buildings have been demolished and replaced with surface parking lots. Heavy traffic and competing big-box retail stores and shopping centers in the outskirts of town have sucked the life out of our city center. Our downtown is no longer friendly to pedestrians or shoppers. What can we do?

Concerned citizens have many reasons for renewing their communities:

- Downtown property owners want to lease vacant properties and halt the decline of real estate values.
- Retailers want more customers.
- Elected officials and business executives understand that younger and older generations (millennials and baby boomers) want to live in vibrant city centers and will move elsewhere if a community does not provide for their needs.
- The public wants to show off its hometown to visitors and take them to an attractive, vibrant downtown.

Fixing Your City addresses these diverse concerns in the following ways:

- It provides conscientious citizens with the information they need to make a difference in their city, and offers solutions to problems that affect local economies and quality of daily life.

- It details a planning process that is affordable and applicable to all cities. Residents of cities tend to think their city is unique. While each city has a particular climate, topography, history, and demographics, and may require tailored solutions for certain issues, I have found that the underlying problems every city faces are essentially the same. The pathway to transformation is universal.

- It provides practical methods for reversing decline and adjusting to the emerging crisis of climate change that are cost-effective, results-oriented, and rooted in the spectacular transformation of Portland, Oregon, in the 1970s. The techniques have evolved over the last forty years from my personal experience as an urban design consultant to cities across the country and my participation in over sixty successful downtown transformation projects.

- It includes innovative urban land use and transportation ideas that have the potential to reduce greenhouse gas emissions. When applied, these ideas can help cities respond to the impacts of climate change.

When I travel to cities across the country in my transformation work I typically hear four basic questions from citizens who are faced with a proposed transformation scheme. Together these questions provide a telling snapshot of the city planning challenges in the United States today:

1. The first question usually comes from a knowledgeable citizen activist who is tired of working hard to create change, but getting no results: "Is this going to be another plan that sits on the shelf, a plan that never gets implemented?"

2. A downtown businessman who thinks he already has the answer to his own question disingenuously asks: "What is the market demand for these proposed interventions?"

3. The third question is commonly delivered in a public meeting from the back of the room by a red-faced gentleman, who stands up and shouts: "Where are you going to get the money to pay for all of these improvements?"

4. Finally, a concerned mother asks: "Is climate change really going to be a problem and is there anything we can do about it?"

The activist is right to be concerned that his or her time will go to waste because most plans end up sitting on the shelf and never get implemented.

The businessman is also right to be concerned about market demand. In most cases, downtowns have deteriorated precisely because businesses no longer want to be there.

The public, too, has a right to be concerned about having sufficient funds for downtown improvements, when there never seems to be enough money to cover even basic needs.

And, finally, the mother's concern about the kind of world she will be leaving her children is one that we all can relate to.

Plans that sit on the shelf are symptomatic of the sorry state of the planning profession today. In most creative endeavors, there is a prescribed process that, if followed, will produce the intended results. Everyone knows that a cook needs to follow the recipe when baking a cake. Leave out a key ingredient and the cake is a failure. The planning process is no different. The problem is that there is no agreed-upon recipe, or process, for producing a successful city plan. *Fixing Your City* addresses this problem by providing a straightforward planning process that guarantees success.

Too frequently, city officials think a market study that assesses existing and future demand for new development will fix an ailing city. Others think a parking strategy will provide the fix. Unfortunately, market studies and solo strategies will do little to create a thriving downtown. The fundamental problem is the downtown has become an unattractive place to visit or do business. Until design plans are prepared that illustrate how to convert a dysfunctional downtown into a place where people want to be, little will change. *Fixing Your City* identifies foolproof procedures that attract businesses back to city centers.

Money is always an issue. At the beginning of the planning process, there seems to be little or none of it available to fund urban improvements. But if a plan is bold and convincing, money will be found. *Fixing Your City* identifies public projects that induce market demand, and describes concrete methods for attracting financial support.

As the need to reduce carbon emissions becomes critical, cities will need to make radical changes to existing plans and policies. *Fixing Your City* identifies actions that mitigate climate change while improving the public's quality of life.

NEW PLANNING MODELS

Fixing Your City introduces new planning models that support city transformation. Together these models constitute the fundamental building blocks for fixing any city:

- The *Transformation Strategy* provides a road map, or process, for a successful transformation journey.

- A *Radical Transformation Strategy* is a research-driven process for addressing big picture and climate change issues.

- *Neighborhood Districts* are the basic building blocks for creating a Transformation Strategy. A neighborhood district can be classified as a *Mobility-Oriented District* (MOD) or a *Bicycle-Oriented District* (BOD). The MOD model is used in population centers where high-capacity transit is available, and the BOD model is used in cities without high-capacity transit. Both models cover an area with a one-mile radius, use protected bikeways to connect residents to neighborhood centers, and reduce reliance on the automobile through design concepts that promote walking, biking, and transit use.

TRANSFORMATION STRATEGY BENEFITS

A Transformation Strategy has the potential to significantly reduce auto emissions by eliminating and shortening auto trips.

In the December 17, 2015, edition of the *New York Times*, a headline read "Despite Push for Cleaner Cars, Sheer Numbers Could Work Against Climate Benefits." The accompanying article stated the following: "Transportation, which is still 95 percent reliant on petroleum, is the world's fastest-growing energy-based contributor to greenhouse gases and about three-quarters of the total comes from motor vehicles." The article claimed that the number of automobiles on the world's roads is on pace to double to more than 2 billion by the year 2030, and that experts predict most of those additional cars will have internal combustion engines, which burn carbon-emitting gasoline or diesel fuels.

Electric vehicles, the article went on to say, are expected to contribute very little towards the reduction of greenhouse gas emissions. In the United States, the short distance between charges will limit their use—while in much of the developing world, electricity will come from coal-fired power plants that are themselves among the planet's biggest emitters of carbon dioxide.

The article sadly concluded that there are no good solutions for significantly reducing global automobile emissions—the benefits of improved fuel efficiencies and electric cars will be more than offset by the additional one billion cars expected on the roads by 2030.

A reduction in automobile emissions from a single neighborhood district will do little to curb global carbon emissions, but if neighborhood districts become the new planning standard, the impact could be enormous.

The challenge is for cities to apply the neighborhood district planning models to retrofit the urban environment. Even if climate change were not a problem, the ability to improve a city's quality of life while stimulating the local economy would make the effort more than worthwhile.

Reducing Automobile Emissions

The two neighborhood district models—the Bicycle-Oriented District (BOD) for cities without high capacity transit (HCT) and the Mobility-Oriented District (MOD) for cities with HCT—are effective means for reducing automobile emissions by integrating land use and transportation concepts that shorten and eliminate automobile trips. They concentrate land uses that generate travel—such as shopping, employment, and recreation—in centers or hubs located within a five-minute bicycle ride on a protected bikeway or within a five-minute walk from the surrounding residential neighborhoods.

The MOD has the potential for reducing automobile emissions by 50% compared to the BOD's 30% reduction, because the MOD is served by transit (light rail, street car, or bus rapid transit) that carries large numbers of passengers, has frequent arrivals and departures, and provides predictable travel times to popular destinations. The BOD is served by buses, which have to contend with the unpredictability of traffic congestion unless traveling in exclusive right-of-way lanes.

The actions required to achieve a 50% reduction in vehicle miles traveled include establishing:

- neighborhood districts
- an enhanced bicycle network through the creation of protected networks that connect neighborhood centers to popular destinations
- an enhanced transit framework, with buses and streetcars in

exclusive right-of-way lanes, that connects neighborhood centers to popular destinations

Applying the neighborhood district planning models to undeveloped areas of a city is not difficult, because roads and buildings haven't been built. Applying the models to developed areas is more challenging, because infrastructure and buildings are in place. The process outlined in this book will help reduce the complexity of applying the models under any circumstance.

Other Benefits

In addition to accommodating growth and reducing automobile emissions, the benefits of a Transformation Strategy for individuals and cities are substantial.

Your Wallet

People who live in neighborhood districts have the potential for more discretionary income by:

- becoming a one-car or no-car household
- reducing their automobile fuel expenditures by up to 50%

Your Health

People in neighborhood districts are healthier because they can leave their cars at home and get more exercise by:

- taking a five-minute walk to their neighborhood center
- taking a five-minute bicycle ride on a protected bikeway to their neighborhood center
- using a bicycle to commute to work

Your Quality of Life

People in neighborhood districts will quite possibly spend less time in their automobile and more time:

- with family and friends
- on recreational activities

Your City

Neighborhood districts offer substantial benefits to cities by providing:

- an annual economic stimulus, often referred to as the green dividend, of up to $50 million for each neighborhood district, thanks to residents driving less, spending less on automobile fuel, and having more discretionary income to spend locally
- more transit riders and increased transit revenues
- reduced road congestion as more people walk, bicycle, and use public transit

Other Issues for Cities

There are a number of other significant issues that can be addressed by a Transformation Strategy, including:

- affordable housing
- gentrification
- homelessness
- equity
- human health
- environmental health
- economic prosperity

NEW TERMINOLOGY

In conjunction with the planning models, a new set of planning terms has emerged:

- The *Business Case* refers to the financial implications associated with a particular land use and transportation plan. It is a valuable decision-making tool for both public officials and private investors.
- *Induced Market Demand* happens when urban design proposals create demand for development in locations that investors have avoided.
- *Game Changers* are public projects that stimulate development momentum. Every Transformation Strategy should include game changers—without them success will be limited. Typical Game Changers are parks, plazas, and street improvements that attract the public and investment.

- *Urban Design Fundamentals* are design requirements essential to the successful location and design of public and private urban improvements.

- *Response Sheets* are ballots that quantify public support for proposed urban design schemes and generate public support when used during the planning process. A typical Response Sheet may contain up to twenty proposed schemes, along with the means for a "yes," "no," or "other" response.

- *Silver Bullets* are projects that harm the city. They propose a cure for an ailing city, but are the product of "magical thinking," and typically end up making things worse. For a city to remain healthy, it is important to dodge Silver Bullets. A plan to reduce automobile congestion on a roadway by removing parking and narrowing or eliminating sidewalks, for example, would be considered a Silver Bullet.

- *Planning Placebos* are planning exercises with little long-term value. They are popular with professional planners because outcomes are seldom controversial. Planning placebos can be expensive, time-consuming, and generally offer little return on the investment of public funds. Like any placebo, they do no real harm, but they are a poor substitute for an effective Transformation Strategy. A visual preference survey would be considered a planning placebo.

- *Shelf Plans* never get implemented. The primary reason is the planning profession's failure to develop informed urban design alternatives.

CHAPTER ONE

Our Cities Need Help

Cities become undesirable places to live and invest in when effective plans to shape growth and development are lacking and short-term economic interests control decision-making.

As a young architect just out of school, I was excited to begin working in the Portland office of Skidmore, Owings & Merrill (SOM), a firm with a fine national and international reputation. I'd been hired as an architect, but in time I started working on some of the larger planning projects in the office. One of the most important was the Environmental Impact Study (EIS) for the proposed Mt. Hood Freeway—an ill-conceived proposal to build a freeway through the heart of Portland's southeast residential neighborhoods. This experience became definitive for my personal development as an architect and urban designer.

Due to a shortage of workspace, the project team for the freeway study was relegated to another floor of the building. That meant I was constantly taking the elevator between two floors—and cultures—as I had a drafting table in both places: one on the sixteenth floor for my architectural projects; and one on the third floor for the Mt. Hood Freeway project.

Life on the two floors couldn't have been more different. On the sixteenth floor, sitting at long rows of drafting tables under overhead florescent lights, the architects and engineers in their white button-down shirts and conservative ties were bent over boards, pencils in hand, creating office buildings, hospitals, and other large buildings. No one ever talked about how buildings should relate to streets or what the context was for an architectural design.

Downstairs, on the third floor, it was anything but buttoned down. Long hair, colorful shirts, and floor-length skirts for the women were the norm for the thirty or so staff as they pored over maps and reports. The schedule for completing the Environmental Impact Study was particularly tight, and it wasn't unusual to find someone sleeping under a desk when I arrived in the morning.

Downstairs there was always lots of lively discussion. Specialized consultants—transportation engineers, landscape architects, air quality and acoustic engineers, historians, and economists—added their diverse views and expertise to the mix. Our team was passionate about trying to save Portland's eastside neighborhoods from the destructive impacts of the freeway. If built, the freeway would have destroyed 1,700 homes, displaced 5,000 people, and eliminated 1,900 jobs. Our EIS findings indicated that the freeway would not relieve congestion and that it would be obsolete when completed. These findings were devastating and definitive—the project was shelved.

Upstairs, I learned about the fine art of designing a building. Downstairs, I learned to appreciate the complex forces that shape our cities.

FAILING CITIES

Cities are always changing. Populations expand and contract. New businesses arrive and others leave. Large employers go out of business as the demand for their products wanes due to changing markets or domestic and foreign competition. Big-box stores on the edge of downtown suck the life out of the downtown retail core. New highways create opportunities for development on the edge of a city that compete with downtown businesses. Cities change for many reasons. In most cases, their downtowns suffer.

Though cities come in all sizes, their problems are universal. Growing towns and cities all have to deal with automobile congestion and the demand for affordable housing. Cities that are losing population have to contend with shrinking revenues and a diminishing ability to provide public services. If these and other problems are ignored, a city will continue to degrade.

Cities are like buildings. They need to be updated from time to time. At the most basic level, if infrastructure—roads, water, and sewer systems—is not maintained, the city becomes an undesirable place in which to live and do business. In addition to basic maintenance tasks, cities need programs to attract employment and keep retail healthy. They should provide public amenities such as parks and open space, promote a wide range of housing choices, support high-quality education, and encourage the development of cultural and entertainment facilities.

With all of these competing demands, the primary question for every city is where to spend scarce public funds. What are the projects or programs that will be the most beneficial? What public improvements will attract the best private investment and improve the quality of life? *Answers to these and many other questions can be answered by creating a Transformation Strategy.* This is the essential tool for fixing a city—whether large or small, whether losing or gaining population. An effective Transformation Strategy eliminates guesswork and guides decision-making about spending priorities and critical interventions.

How Cities Deteriorate

Before attempting to solve a city's problems, it is helpful to have an understanding of how its physical character eroded over time. Then, solutions for correcting the situation can be developed. Typically, most problems faced by cities result from (1) a depletion of the retail offering, (2) the creation of a hostile pedestrian environment, and (3) the preponderance of visual blight and chaos.

Depleted Retail Offerings

- Strip malls, big-box stores, and shopping centers located outside of the city center diminish the downtown's economic vitality and force many retailers to close shop.

- The downtown retail environment is further weakened as non-retail uses such as real estate offices, law offices, and exercise studios move into vacant ground-floor space once occupied by shops and other retail enterprises.

- Retail buildings are demolished to make way for new banks, office buildings, and surface parking lots.

- More traffic lanes are added and curbside parking for the convenience of retail customers is removed, further discouraging shopping.

- Retail-friendly two-way streets are changed to one-way streets to accommodate more automobile traffic.

Hostile Pedestrian Environment

- Sidewalks are narrowed to allow for additional lanes of traffic, thereby reducing the space available for outdoor retail displays, benches, restaurant seating, and side-by-side walking.

- Curbside parking is removed, and physical separation between pedestrians and moving traffic is lacking, which makes pedestrians feel unsafe.

- Intersections are widened, increasing the crossing distances for pedestrians.

- Automated pedestrian traffic signals are replaced by push button signals, which frustrate pedestrians who want to cross a street without asking for permission.

- Surface parking lots, drive-through banking facilities, and faceless office facades replace retail storefronts, further degrading the walking experience.

- Large civic structures, such as government offices, arenas, and convention centers with ground-level blank walls, are built in the center of downtown, creating an environment that feels unsafe.

Visual Blight and Chaos

- Historic facades are covered with cheap, trendy building materials.
- Unique historic buildings are demolished and replaced with characterless modern buildings.
- New buildings are constructed next to landmark historic buildings without consideration of design compatibility.
- Placeless structures that don't reflect regional character, climate conditions, or social values are built.
- Oversized, garish, and inappropriately placed signage creates further visual blight.

Not Every City Can Be Fixed

I am often asked if downtowns with a depleted retail offering and a hostile pedestrian environment can be salvaged. In some cases, the answer is *no*, because there are just too many buildings that have inactive ground floors. For example, many buildings may have blank walls or excessive building setbacks from the public sidewalk. Some buildings may be parking structures that lack commercial activity at the ground level. These are sometimes referred to as bunker buildings, and often cannot be renovated due to floor elevations that don't match adjacent sidewalks, interior spaces not suited to commercial uses, or prohibitive remodeling costs. If a downtown has too many bunker buildings, its situation may be terminal.

Terminal downtowns are legion in the United States and Canada. Obviously, there's always something that can be done to improve any downtown, but in most cases isolated bunker building improvements don't really make a meaningful difference. *The challenge for cities is to take steps to prevent bunker buildings from being built in the first place.*

The Ultimate Yardstick

From time to time, urban design pundits like to identify what they consider to be the worst-designed cities in the world. Atlanta, Jakarta, and Sao Paulo are frequently singled out for this dubious distinction.

These cities have serious problems stemming from the absence of planning, too much congestion, and urban sprawl.

At the same time, everyone has a favorite city. In Europe it might be Florence or Barcelona. In the United States, it may be Savannah or Santa Fe. In Canada, many people love Quebec City and Vancouver. All these cities have one thing in common—they are pedestrian-friendly.

Though it may seem an oversimplification to evaluate a city in terms of its pedestrian experience, the fact is that the public's yardstick for what constitutes a favorite city is how it feels to walk down the streets of that city. Invariably, desirable places are pedestrian-friendly.

If the pedestrian experience is so fundamental to creating a desirable city, why don't more cities take action to protect and enhance the pedestrian arena? Regrettably, the reason is that the automobile has become the primary force shaping our cities. And the automobile has voracious demands for convenient access, bigger roads, and more parking. Satisfying those demands has become the top priority for most city transportation engineers. *Replacing the automobile with the pedestrian as the top priority is the fundamental first step for any city that is serious about transformation.*

FLAWED PLANS

Commonly, when I visit a city for the first time, people say, "We've been planning for years and nothing ever changes. We don't want another plan that sits on the shelf!"

The public's perception is right. Too few transformation plans are implemented or result in tangible change. Flawed plans can be attributed to an arbitrary planning process, a lack of public involvement, failure to address implementation, or the adoption of planning placebos. Problems may also stem from the planning professionals' limited experience, the lack of money, or a failure to develop informed design alternatives.

Flaws in the Planning Process

An Arbitrary Planning Process

As strange as it may seem, there are few standardized procedures for preparing a city Transformation Strategy. If you asked a group of planners to describe the procedure for preparing and implementing such a plan, each would have a different answer. In other professions, such as law, medicine, or architecture, clear procedures have evolved and are followed.

Architects, for example, have a specific set of steps they go through to design a building and have it constructed. The American Institute of Architects (AIA) defines standardized procedures for the full range of services that an architect provides. This makes it easy for both the client and the architect to agree on services and to measure the progress of a project. Both parties agree on what it takes to move from the drawing board to a finished building. The process, which is logical and results-oriented, includes discrete phases: schematic design, design development, preparation of contract documents, and contract administration.

The comparable professional organization for planners, the American Planning Association (APA), does not provide a similar set of guidelines. There are no standardized processes for planning professionals to adhere to, nor any standardized procedures and contractual forms. Consequently, agreements between professional planners and their clients often lack clarity. In the absence of nationwide standards, "shelf plans" have proliferated across the country.

The confusion surrounding how planners conduct their work is often reflected in Requests for Proposals (RFPs), which are sent out to planning firms when a city agency or other client seeks professional planning assistance.

Typically, an RFP includes a scope of work and a budget. However, there are no standard guidelines for what a scope of work should include. Some clients want a verbal vision, or narrative, that will describe a way to change their city. Other clients prefer a process that entails analyzing and salvaging parts of previously discarded "shelf plans," with the expectation that a better solution will emerge. Still other clients want a planning firm to develop a set of detailed standards or codes for the city, while the fundamental design work for establishing the rationales for the codes is ignored. A client may seek a solution based on a detailed market study that identifies specific types of new development with the hopes that the free market will respond accordingly and the ideal project will be built. Another popular, though woefully misguided approach, is that a city's problems can be resolved by simply commissioning a study that addresses parking deficiencies. There are even clients who believe that the creation of a branding campaign for a city is the key to transformation. Unfortunately, none of these approaches will get the job done.

Unrealistic Planning Horizons

It's not uncommon that a city planning director will want a twenty-five-year plan. While there is nothing inherently wrong with looking ahead that far into the future, it is unlikely that anyone who prepares or advocates for a twenty-five-year plan will be around for such a long length of time.

A twenty-five-year plan is an invitation to do nothing in the short term, assuming that someone will take care of things at a later date. A phased plan that gives highest priority to the initial five-year phase is a better alternative. If momentum is not well-established in the first five years, the plan has little chance for success.

Timid Plans

Timid plans are a product of inexperienced planners and consultants. They contain vague and ineffective proposals. Good plans contain bold interventions that solve fundamental problems. A robust strategy that captures the imagination of the public and key decision-makers is easier to implement.

Planning Vacuum

In the absence of a plan, real-estate developers are often able to convince decision-makers to approve projects that are not in the community's best interest. Why is that? In the short term their projects can create jobs and increase tax revenues, but, too often, the longer-term reality is just the opposite—their projects, due to location or design, end up making city transformation even more difficult to achieve.

Lack of Follow-through

A common misconception in the world of planning is that once a plan is finished, implementation will simply happen of its own accord. Actually, implementation won't happen if it is left up to city staff and elected officials. Elected officials come and go, and city staff does not have the political muscle needed to get things done. Implementation will only happen if a committee of influential citizens is appointed by city officials to oversee and drive the implementation process.

Inadequate or Ineffective Public Involvement

Most everyone agrees that public involvement in the planning process is a good thing. However, the quality and effectiveness of the public's participation in the process is not always guaranteed. The crucial factor is whether or not there are meaningful opportunities for the public to contribute to shaping the contents of the plan itself. At a minimum this requires that the public is able to: (1) identify the issues that need to be addressed, (2) select and vote on alternatives for addressing those issues, and (3) review and comment on the implementation strategy.

Unfortunately, in recent years a cottage industry of consultants has emerged that ignores these basic requirements for effective public participation. Not infrequently, pundits like to refer to these public participation programs as public *manipulation* programs, and for good reason. The intention is not to gain useful information, but to convince or sell the public on a preconceived outcome.

Some consultants specialize in keeping the public at bay in order to protect government agencies. Typically, they convene endless meetings that wear the public down. They keep a record of every comment that is made and then give the comments to the planning team to use as it sees fit. Because the public's support, or lack of support, for the various design solutions under consideration has not been determined by a quantifiable vote, the planning team is free to interpret the results in the way that best suits their own preconceived biases and preferred design solutions.

Inattention to Implementation

Typically, urban design plans contain dozens of actions that have been identified for implementation. Too frequently, however, there is no ranking, or hierarchy, of those actions—which to perform first and which to save for later. It is important for public agencies with limited human and financial resources to know whether they can realistically put a plan into action and whether there are sufficient funds for public investments needed to stimulate private development.

As a rule of thumb, an effective Transformation Strategy will identify no more than half a dozen public actions for implementation within the first five years of its adoption. It will single out the most critical implementation actions, or "game changers." And it will provide a financial case to support the investment of public funds in improvements that will stimulate the private sector.

Human Inadequacies

Poorly Trained Professionals

Transforming a city is a complicated undertaking. There are no professional degrees that prepare an individual to understand and deal with the complexities of city transformation. Architects are trained to design buildings on a specific site. Landscape architects design parks and open spaces. City planners develop and administer building codes. None of these professionals are trained to think in a comprehensive way about cities, to integrate the many diverse elements affecting city life, or to design vital, healthy, functional neighborhoods and city centers.

Most cities suffer from ever-increasing automobile traffic, and market forces typically cater to an automobile-centric city. Planners and urban designers have been hard-pressed to come up with effective strategies to counter those destructive trends.

Short-Term Thinking

A let-the-market-decide mentality is a sure formula for creating an unpleasant city. The typical developer is not motivated to think big picture or to take responsibility for being a good neighbor. Developers understand that their financial survival depends on minimizing risks and maximizing profits, so they are likely to favor short-term cookie-cutter projects that provide less exposure to risk than long-term projects requiring customized design. Unfortunately, elected officials and decision-makers tend to defer to developers because they don't want to jeopardize potential tax revenues that developers' projects may generate.

A case in point is the story of a light rail transit (LRT) system that cost millions of dollars in Aurora, Colorado. A local developer who owns hundreds of acres of undeveloped land adjacent to one of the proposed stations was positioned to benefit substantially from the increase in land value due to proximity to the station. In return, the city rightfully expected something from the developer—such as a high-density mixed-use urban project that would contribute to more transit ridership and less automobile travel.

Unfortunately, the local developer rejected all proposals from the city to create a dense, urban-style project. Instead, he made it clear that he preferred a low-density suburban development and that he was reserving a parcel of land for a Walmart store, a prime automobile-dependent destination. This is an example of extreme short-term thinking, intended solely to generate an immediate cash return. The tragedy is that the city of Aurora couldn't fight back, because it did not have the necessary codes and standards in place to promote development solutions consistent with the public's investment in the LRT system.

Insufficient Experience and Expertise

Elected officials are seldom aware of what it takes to transform a city or town. Typically, they rely on a local planning director to inform them about what needs to be done. In my experience, it is unusual to encounter a planning director who has had prior experience with preparing an effective transformation plan. In the absence of leadership and experience, piecemeal planning efforts are undertaken.

Silo Thinking

Governmental organizations are prone to silo thinking. Land-use planners are typically at odds with transportation planners, and high-capacity transit agencies often see things differently than bus agencies. Without a mechanism for integrating these diverse perspectives, the potential benefits of strategies coordinated to address critical issues are lost.

The Role of Money

Scarce Financial Resources

Many cities try to produce a transformation plan on the cheap. This becomes apparent when a city agency releases a Request for Proposal (RFP) without including a budget. The omission is another way of saying, *Tell us what you charge, and we'll give the job to the lowest bidder.* A city that sincerely seeks to hire a consultant to produce an effective plan will establish a reasonable budget up front and make it available to all concerned.

A successful transformation project inevitably requires public expenditure on infrastructure in order to attract private investment. If funds for infrastructure are not available, transformation will be difficult.

Overrated Market Studies

Cities often retain economists to identify market demand and the types of businesses they might attract. The thinking is that city boosters can use market surveys to attract new business. There is a problem with this approach: businesses who aren't interested in coming to a city before a market survey won't be attracted to it afterwards, unless significant changes are made in the urban environment.

Market-demand studies are not magic. The estimates they provide are directly proportional to the size of the population, anticipated population growth, and the availability of existing services. What market studies overlook is vital information about *where* new development should be located and *how* it should be configured to be of the most benefit.

The story of Lincoln, Nebraska, illustrates this point. My firm had been retained to prepare a downtown Transformation Strategy. The city had retained a national economics firm to prepare a market study for Antelope Valley, a neighborhood adjacent to the downtown. The study concluded that there was sufficient market demand in Antelope Valley to warrant building a major retail center. But we were concerned. We understood that the proposed Antelope Valley retail development would absorb all the demand for new retail construction for years to come, and, as a result, downtown retailers would suffer. We recommended shelving the Antelope Valley proposal in order to strengthen the downtown—the heart of the city. Fortunately for Lincoln, our recommendations were adopted.

The question for every city is this: *If there's a demand for retail, why isn't it showing up in downtown?* In most cases the answer is because the downtown's retail offering is degraded and there is no perceived potential for changing the situation. An effective Transformation Strategy that configures a unique, pedestrian-friendly shopping environment can resolve these problems.

For market demand studies to be effective, they need to part of a larger planning effort, and they need to illustrate how a strategy will create market demand and stimulate the local economy.

Overlooking the Importance of Design

Flawed Designs

Understanding how to design the fundamental features of a city to ensure its success is the first step in transformation. It is not unusual for a consultant team to propose flawed urban design solutions because they do not understand the fundamental requirements described in Chapter Four.

Visioning

There is a plethora of visioning specialists who offer all manner of activities designed to identify the public's aspirations. Typically, they engage the public in a variety of complicated exercises strung out over a period of several months. Unfortunately, the outcomes of these activities typically lack specificity and so could be used in just about any city. Everybody everywhere wants clean air and water, safe streets, good schools, and a strong economy. There's nothing unique about such preferences, so the final vision document will end up having limited value in producing a robust Transformation Strategy.

Such visioning exercises become bloated, expensive undertakings, and the information they provide is difficult to translate into effective plans and policies. It is preferable to establish a fixed budget before the visioning process begins to make sure it constitutes only a small percentage of the total planning budget. At the onset of a project, a method for tabulating and integrating the findings from the visioning process into the final plan should be established.

Vague Design Solutions

A typical city plan is generally heavy on words and policies but short on graphics that realistically illustrate proposed design solutions. It's not uncommon to find a 100-page planning report with only two or three pages of illustrations.

Plans should be full of drawings illustrating proposed design concepts. Wordy plans are intimidating and seldom read. On the other hand, well-illustrated plans are accessible and effective.

Visual Preference Surveys

Visual preference surveys consist of images of proposed construction projects that are presented to the public in order to determine community preferences. Not surprisingly, the public always prefers beautiful, intimate projects to those that are ugly and impersonal. Comparing a strip shopping mall to a pedestrian-friendly shopping street invariably provides predictable results, as critics of visual preference surveys like to point out. In the end, these generic and predictable results are of little meaningful value in preparing an effective plan.

Charrettes

A charrette is a collaborative planning process. Charrettes can last one day or several days. They bring the public together in intensive work sessions to design, critique, and refine design solutions that respond to public concerns. Traditionally, a third-party facilitator runs a charrette session. There are a number of fundamental problems with charrettes, including the lack of talent for developing credible design solutions on the spot and insufficient time to produce defensible design solutions.

Walk-Arounds

Some public agencies like to use walk-arounds, or walking tours, to involve the public in the planning process. These generally happen at the beginning of a project. The public is invited to join a tour of the planning area and discuss issues. During the walk, the public is encouraged to take photographs of places and features they find important. The participants' feedback and photographs are then posted online but are rarely used.

Branding

Some cities believe that the pathway to success is simply a matter of hiring branding specialists and promoting the city with the right brand. This is an expensive process, and there is little evidence to suggest that brand names make much of a difference. Especially when a high-quality pedestrian environment with shopping and entertainment opportunities is not already available, the branding exercise can be a wasted effort.

Case Studies

Many planning projects require an extensive review of case studies and literature describing similar projects. While the descriptions of other projects may make for interesting reading, they are seldom applicable to the situation at hand. A healthy dose of skepticism should be part of any such review.

Developer Offerings

Many cities try to stimulate economic development with stand-alone development projects. For example, a city will retain an economist to identify a piece of land in the downtown that could be attractive to developers. An offering package along with promotional information is prepared. The project is advertised, development proposals are received and evaluated, and a developer is selected to build the project. In these situations, it is customary for the city to provide financial incentives to make the offering package attractive to the development community.

However, serious developers want to know what types of projects and interventions are being planned for the future in surrounding neighborhoods, in order to minimize their risks. They are most interested in development offerings in cities that have adopted a downtown Transformation Strategy. As one developer summarized it to me, "I am only interested in cities that have decided what they want to be when they grow up."

Code Rewrites

Some cities try to shortcut the planning process by developing a vision, and then writing regulations or codes to implement the vision. They skip the design phase altogether and do not identify where specific land uses should be located, or how people will move through the urban area. They ignore projects that will improve the quality of life, or projects that will stimulate the local economy. This approach is a recipe for a failed city.

CLIMATE CHANGE

Fixing Your City explains how to prepare an effective city Transformation Strategy and includes innovative land use and transportation solutions that have the potential to significantly reduce greenhouse gas emissions. These principles provide the fundamental planning tools every city needs to respond to climate change.

The consequences of climate change are substantial.

Sea-Level Changes

In the future, coastal cities can expect significant impact from rising sea levels. Though the amount and rate of rise is not known with certainty, the fact is that sea levels *will* rise.

James Hansen, a renowned climate activist, described the issue in his 2013 publication *Assessing Dangerous Climate Change:*

The important point is that the uncertainty is not about whether continued rapid CO_2 emissions would cause large sea level rise, submerging coastlines—it is about how soon the large changes would begin. The carbon from fossil fuel burning will remain in and affect the climate system for many millennia, ensuring that over time sea level rise of many meters will occur—tens of meters if most of the fossil fuels are burned. That level of sea level rise would result in the loss of hundreds of historical coastal cities worldwide with incalculable economic consequences, create hundreds of millions of global warming refugees from highly-populated low-lying areas, and thus likely cause international conflicts.

Severe Weather Events

Warming oceans will produce heavy rainfall and more devastating hurricanes, flooding low-lying coastal areas.

Health Threat

"The human symptoms of climate change are unequivocal and potentially irreversible," a recent report by the British medical journal the *Lancet* says. The situation is so serious that significant gains by modern medicine and technology are being undercut.

Some of the findings of the *Lancet Countdown on Health and Climate Change* report:

- *Increased Disease:* Climate change "is the major health threat of the twenty-first century." Warming is exacerbating the spread of Dengue fever, the world's most rapidly expanding disease. Dengue is a virus spread by mosquitoes, and can result in fever, headaches, and pain. Severe cases can bring a multitude of symptoms, including bleeding, shock, organ failure—and potentially death. There is no treatment or vaccine.

- *Air Pollution:* Global exposure to dangerous levels of air pollution has increased. More than 2,100 cities globally exceed recommended levels of atmospheric particulate matter—particles emitted when fuels, such as coal or diesel, are burned, and are small enough to get into lungs. Pollution was linked to nine million deaths worldwide in 2015.

16

- *Heat Stress:* The elderly are most vulnerable to high-temperature extremes. Temperatures and the frequency of extremes are increasing. With populations now living longer, the numbers of those vulnerable to heat stresses will only go up.

"The delayed response to climate change over the past twenty-five years has jeopardized human health and livelihoods," the report says. The direct effects of climate change "result from rising temperatures and changes in the frequency and strength of storms, floods, droughts, and heatwaves," and "have physical and mental health consequences."

Economy

Once-rare weather events are becoming stronger and more frequent. The UN's International Labor Organization says that people who depend heavily on natural resources will be the hardest hit.

In the Caribbean where 2.3 million people are employed in the $35 billion tourism industry, the 2017 hurricane devastation caused canceled reservations, delivering a major blow to the economy. It may take years to recover; indeed, recovery is not assured.

Other employment sectors are being impacted. The agricultural industry is being hit hard by climate extremes. Fire and drought are taking a toll worldwide. The fishing industry is in peril as ocean acidification destroys fish populations.

A consequence of climate change may be a temporary employment boom remaking damaged cities and disaster-proofing others. These repair activities may not be sustainable, as there will be limits on how much the public is willing to spend to fix what is broken.

Mass Migrations

Among the many devastating impacts cities and regions will experience with rising temperatures are failing crops and food shortages, water shortages, and mass migrations from areas that become uninhabitable because of heat.

Mitigating the Impacts of Climate Change

In light of these pressing issues, every city must ask what it can do to reduce carbon emissions. New concepts introduced in this book provide the means for cities to effectively address this question. The neighborhood district planning models have the potential to improve the quality of life in the city while reducing automobile use by up to half, which will in turn help reduce carbon emissions. The Transformation Strategy uses the neighborhood district planning models to enable cities to respond quickly and effectively to the consequences of a rapidly changing world.

TRANSPORTATION EMISSIONS

The US transportation sector is responsible for about a third of our country's climate-changing emissions. Reducing transportation emissions is a critical step in fighting climate change. There is an imperative to shift away from fossil-fuel vehicle dependence and the suburban sprawl that accompanies it—and toward alternative fuels, public transportation, and better land-use patterns, reducing our country's total vehicle miles traveled each year.

Indications are that emerging technologies allowing ride-hailing and self-driving cars will increase rather than decrease carbon emissions.

Autonomous Vehicle (AV)

Automobile manufacturers would have us believe that self-driving vehicles—Autonomous Vehicles (AV)—will be good for everyone. They are enthusiastic about the benefits. They suggest that we will no longer need our own cars. We can be relieved of costly automobile ownership expenses. We can avoid collisions. We will not need a garage. We can have a bigger front lawn because the driveway will not be needed. When you need a car, just dial a number and within minutes one will appear at your front door. If you are going to your place of employment you can read or daydream along the way. When you arrive, you will not need to worry about locating or paying for a parking space. Just get out, and the car will disappear down the road. These are just a few of the possibilities we hear about.

Recently the transportation planning firm Fehr & Peers published a paper testing how AVs might change the predicted outcomes of seven travel models, in regions around the US. All results were comparisons to future condition without any AVs. Key findings:

- Vehicle Miles Traveled (VMT) increased in all seven models (range of +12% to +68%) when assuming no regulatory requirements for ridesharing.

- Regulations requiring half of AV trips to be shared would help mitigate the VMT increase, but would not fully offset it.
- Total transit trips declined in five of the seven models tested by a range of -8% to -43%. The two others showed increased transit trips of 5% to 16%.
- Of the four models for which specific types of transit trips were tested, three showed declines ranging from 26% to 47% for bus trips and 13% to 40% for rail trips.

These results are not good news for efforts to reduce carbon emissions. Concerns include:

Increased Carbon Emissions

Reducing carbon emissions requires significant decreases in VMT. AVs significantly increased VMT in all models by 12–68%.

More Congestion

Congestion plagues our cities now. AVs add to congestion by increasing VMT by 12–68%.

Less Transit Use

The most energy-efficient way to travel is on public transit. AVs reduced bus trips by 26–47% and rail trips by 13–40%. A reduction in transit use would severely strain transit systems—forcing many agencies to close or reduce service.

Electric Cars

2017 has been characterized as the beginning of the end of the internal combustion engine. Recently Volvo, Volkswagen, Mercedes, Audi, BMW, and Ford have all announced plans to build electric vehicles (EV). The potential benefits in terms of reduced carbon emissions are substantial.

Depending on how electricity is produced in a region, electric cars are 30–80% lower in greenhouse gas emissions, according to Gina Coplon-Newfield, the director of the Sierra Club's Electric Vehicle

Initiative. The emission reductions are most significant in the Pacific Northwest, where a large percentage of power is generated by renewables (hydro and wind), and least in the Midwest, where power is heavily reliant on power generated with fossil fuels.

Electric cars are a positive development in efforts to reduce carbon emissions, but experts predict that a future in which electric cars are the norm is still years away. And electric cars do nothing to reduce congestion.

Ride-hailing

Ride-hailing services (like Uber and Lyft) contribute to growth in vehicle miles traveled and shift trips away from more sustainable modes, such as public transit, biking, and walking. This disturbing trend means more congestion in cities, and more carbon emissions.

New York has already been impacted by ride-hailing. Congestion has increased and transit ridership and revenues have fallen as travelers substitute ride-hailing services for transit.

Autonomous Rapid Transit (ART)

Autonomous rapid transit (ART) uses AV technology in small express buses traveling in auto-free lanes. Like bus rapid transit (BRT) in auto-free lanes, it has the potential to reduce VMT by eliminating auto trips.

Reducing VMT

To counter emerging technologies that increase VMT and carbon emissions, decision-makers need to adopt plans and policies that give priority to all forms of high-capacity transit (HCT) in auto-free lanes. HCT includes heavy rail, light rail transit (LRT), BRT, ART, and streetcars. When HCT is used in combination with congestion pricing and an integrated land use strategy, the potential for reducing carbon emissions and congestion is significant. (See Chapter Seven.)

CHAPTER TWO

Transformation Strategy

Successful plans are a product of a systematic planning process.

It was the mid-1980s, and Portland was growing fast, so the City Council decided that it was time to update the 1972 Downtown Plan. A fifteen-person Steering Committee composed of representatives from various special-interest groups was charged with leading the planning effort. The group was diverse, with representatives from labor, business, low-income housing, minority communities, and neighborhoods. Two key political appointees were the Chairman of the Steering Committee, an architect; and the project's Plan Manager, an attorney. Neither had any experience developing a central city plan.

The city hired me to lead a four-person Urban Design Advisory Team to guide the planning effort. We walked right into trouble—big trouble. Our Urban Design Advisory Team recommended that as a first step a systematic planning process be adopted. The Chairman of the Steering Committee rejected our recommendation, as he felt a planning process would restrict the Steering Committee's creative efforts. In fact, the Committee didn't want any advice or counsel at all from the Urban Design Advisory Team—they felt that our experience might bias them.

The Steering Committee was keen to get lots of public input, so they asked citizens to "give us your dreams." The public responded with over 10,000 dreams! Unfortunately, a process for sorting and interpreting all those wonderful dreams had not been established, and so the information gathered—at great public expense—was of little use.

Without a defined planning process, the project began to flounder. The budget was seriously depleted, and the project was way behind schedule.

The Mayor and City Council began to understand the seriousness of the situation when local newspapers published articles about the dysfunctional planning effort.

A newly elected City Commissioner was assigned to manage the project. In a hastily arranged meeting, his staff said to me, "We have a problem. Our commissioner has inherited a turkey. How do we get it off his plate?" I recommended that the Steering Committee should be thanked for their involvement and dismissed immediately, and that the responsibility for completing the project then be turned over to the city's Planning Bureau. Very little could be salvaged from the incomplete work—the best they could do was to produce a seriously compromised plan as quickly as possible and get it off the table. The tragedy was that the potential for a bold, progressive plan was never realized. In the end, time, money, and opportunity had been squandered.

This maddening, frustrating episode taught me a very significant lesson: it is absolutely imperative to have a systematic planning process and experienced leadership in place before the planning begins.

Implementation Rules
Policies, Regulations, and Design Guidelines

Framework Plan
Retail, Employment, Housing, Civic Uses,
Open Space, Complete Streets,
Implementation

Public Support

Transformation Strategy Basic Elements

A SYSTEMATIC PLANNING PROCESS

After many years preparing and reviewing plans for cities, I became interested in why some plans were successful and others were not. In order to determine what exactly worked for cities and what didn't, I decided to evaluate the plans that my firm had created, along with the plans of other consultants.

I discovered, to my dismay, that far too many plans were flawed and ended up sitting on a shelf. We needed a deeper understanding of what worked to bring about positive change, and what didn't.

The few plans that did produce significant results were *reader-friendly*, and included a strong *emphasis on physical design*. They also contained an implementation program that produced substantial momentum for change *within the first five years* of the plan's adoption as well as *strategically located public investments*. Lastly, I discovered that if a city didn't establish *guidelines and standards* to support their recommendations, fundamental concepts of the plan would be seriously compromised.

The most common problem with the unsuccessful plans was the lack of a systematic planning process. To address that void, I developed a three-part strategy for transformation, which I call a Transformation

Strategy. It incorporates everything I've learned over the course of my professional life and offers a clear, direct, and reliable pathway to successful urban transformation. All three parts of the Transformation Strategy process are essential, and if one or two parts are left out, the planning effort will not result in robust, long-lasting transformation.

Like a house, the three basic elements of the Transformation Strategy provide a foundation, an enclosure, and a roof.

Public support provides the foundation for the Transformation Strategy. The Framework Plan provides an enclosure for the transformation design elements and interventions, and the implementation rules provide a roof to protect the integrity of the completed Framework Plan. A Transformation Strategy, much like a house, will not survive if any one of the three components is missing.

A Transformation Strategy is different than a typical downtown master plan. Most often a master plan is a wordy document with generalized land-use concepts and very little information about next steps. A Transformation Strategy is very detailed, with an emphasis on the built environment and public improvements that will generate immediate transformation momentum by attracting private investment.

Part One: Public Support

A Transformation Strategy involves a public-involvement process that is economical and effective. It educates the public about the transformation process and creates a constituency for developing and implementing the Transformation Strategy.

Part Two: Framework Plan

The Framework Plan is the heart of a Transformation Strategy. If the design element is weak, the Transformation Strategy will not succeed. It will become a shelf plan. Land use/circulation actions required to make necessary interventions are identified. Typically, the time required to complete a Framework Plan is approximately six to nine months.

Part Three: Implementation Rules

Implementation rules outline essential guidelines and standards to ensure that the intent of the Framework Plan is achieved. These rules tend to be the missing component in most planning efforts, yet they are an essential requirement if a Transformation Strategy is to be successful. Implementation rules include public area standards, development regulations, design guidelines, and a design review process.

A detailed description of each of the three parts of a Transformation Strategy can be found in Chapters Three, Four, and Five.

Phases for the Framework Plan

There are three phases of work in producing a Framework Plan.

Phase 1: Start

The focus of the start phase is to identify the most important community issues to be addressed in the development of the Framework Plan.

Too often, consultants and their clients become fixated on analyzing and summarizing stale information that was generated in previous planning studies, and therefore end up spending far too much time in the start phase. Though it may be tempting to draw on the findings of a previous plan, outdated material is rarely, if ever, valuable in producing an effective Framework Plan.

It is not uncommon for 60% of a project's budget to be allocated to the start phase—but the start phase, including public support, should consume no more than 20% of the budget.

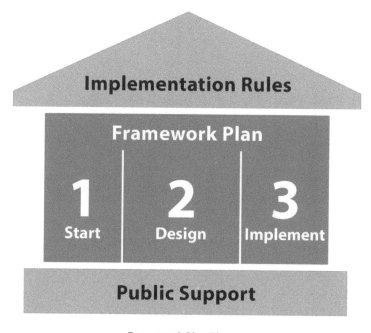

Framework Plan Phases

Phase 2: Design

The second phase is the most important part of the Framework Plan. During the design phase, alternative possibilities for responding to the community's issues are developed and evaluated, and the best alternatives are selected and refined.

The major portion of any Framework Plan budget—at least 60%—should be allocated to the design phase. But it's not uncommon to see less than 30% of a project budget allocated to this task.

Many Framework Plans lose focus during the design phase. This is often due to insufficient talent and experience on the part of the consultant team and an inability to deal with the complexities of a Framework Plan. Architects and professional planners are, at times, of little help. Architects are schooled in the design of individual buildings on particular sites—not necessarily in the complex configuration of multi-building projects or entire segments of a city. Planners are trained to address rules and regulations and may have little exposure to or understanding of urban design. The vacuum created by the absence of sufficient design expertise can produce an ineffective Framework Plan. The challenge for every city is to find consultants with the adequate experience and training to produce a successful, highly effective Framework Plan.

For the design phase to be successful, it is vital that the project team includes experienced professionals, who have:

- demonstrable design talent
- an awareness of urban design solutions that are successful
- competency in developing creative solutions
- experience preparing graphic materials for community review—materials that can be easily understood by the general public

It is also important that members of the project team stay open to all possibilities, so that the best solutions can emerge.

Phase 3: Implement

A plan is only as good as its implementation strategy. The implementation phase constitutes the bottom line in any planning process.

Too often the implementation strategy is an afterthought, and given only 5–10% of a project's budget. A more appropriate budget allocation for the implementation phase is on the order of 20% of the Framework Plan budget.

The implementation portion of a Framework Plan is the roadmap to success, and should address the following issues:

- Is the strategy for implementation clear?
- What are the plan's priorities?
- What are the game-changing projects?
- What is the business case (return on investment) for the proposed public improvements?
- Are responsibilities clearly defined and funding strategies well-developed?

SHELF PLANS

The Transformation Strategy systematic planning process produces plans that get implemented. Shelf plans don't get implemented. In shelf plans the Framework Plan is anemic or missing. Instead, the emphasis is on never-ending public involvement and arbitrary implementation rules.

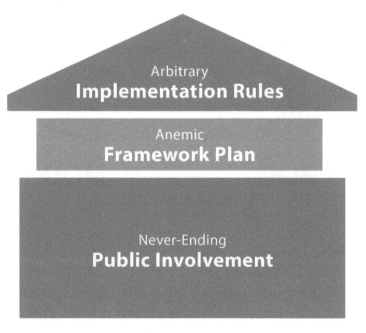

Shelf Plan Characteristics

NEIGHBORHOOD DISTRICTS

Because of the urgency of climate change and the imperative to reduce carbon emissions, our firm has focused on developing new land-use/transportation models that have the potential to significantly alter the relationship between where people live and how they travel for work and commerce.

Since our goal was to reduce reliance on the automobile, we studied the various purposes for travel. We learned that most daily trips are for work, shopping, and recreation. We could see that if households are located in close proximity to these daily destinations, automobile trips would be shortened. And if households are located within a five-minute walk, or a safe five-minute bicycle ride, many automobile trips could be eliminated altogether.

By using the above parameters to shorten or eliminate automobile trips, we developed two new planning models that illustrate scenarios for achieving significant energy savings as well as economic benefits.

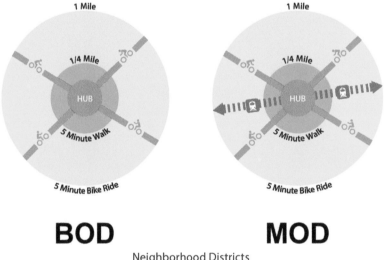

BOD   **MOD**

Neighborhood Districts

BOD and MOD

Both the Bicycle-Oriented District (BOD) and Mobility-Oriented District (MOD) models include protected bikeways that connect the surrounding residential areas to a hub. The BOD may or may not include bus transit. The MOD includes High Capacity Transit (HCT)—such as a streetcar, light rail, or bus rapid transit. HCT's reliability and ability to carry large passenger loads offers the greatest potential for reducing automobile travel.

These models differ from traditional planning models in many important ways.

Integration of Land Use and Transportation

Both the BOD and MOD neighborhood models are organized around a central hub with a grocery store, restaurants, and retail and commercial services. The ideal hub also contains employment opportunities. All neighborhood residents live within a five-minute bicycle ride of the hub, and many residents live within a five-minute walk of the hub. The BOD is served by buses on streets, and the MOD is served by BRT, LRT, or streetcar.

Larger Impact Area

Traditional neighborhood planning models encompass an area up to a quarter- or half-mile in distance from the neighborhood center. The BOD and MOD models, on the other hand, encompass an area extending one mile from the center of a hub. That's an increase in acreage sixteen times greater than the amount of land encompassed by the traditional quarter-mile planning model.

Features of a Neighborhood District

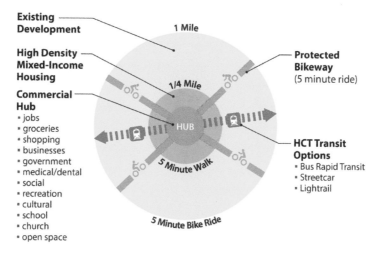

Neighborhood District (MOD)

The Commercial Hub

A commercial hub containing all the shopping, recreational, and employment opportunities needed to serve the surrounding residential neighborhoods is a vital part of a neighborhood district.

In both the BOD and MOD models the hub is the centerpiece.

Determining where to locate a hub is the first step in creating a neighborhood district. A hub cannot be located just anywhere; it needs to be located where it has the greatest potential for success.

Questions to consider when locating a hub:

- Is the land area available?
- Can existing land uses be adapted?
- Can the area be served by public transit?
- Can a network of protected bikeways between the hub and adjacent neighborhoods be created?
- Would employers be attracted to the area?
- Can retail be successful in the area?

These issues can be resolved through a conceptual design exercise that determines if a proposed hub location has the necessary potential to supply most of the goods and services needed by residents.

Protected Bikeways

European cities that enjoy high volumes of bicycle riding provide well-protected bicycle lanes for their residents. These protected lanes, sometimes referred to as cycle tracks, are separated from vehicular traffic by physical barriers, such as curbs, landscaping, or parked vehicles. Without the safety a protected bikeway provides, bicycle riders can be expected to comprise less than 10% of all travelers. With protected bikeways, the percentage of all trips made by bicycle could reach as much as 40–50%. On average, a bicycle rider can travel one mile in five minutes on a protected bikeway.

Both the BOD and MOD models include a network of protected bikeways that link surrounding neighborhoods to the central hub, and result in less automobile usage.

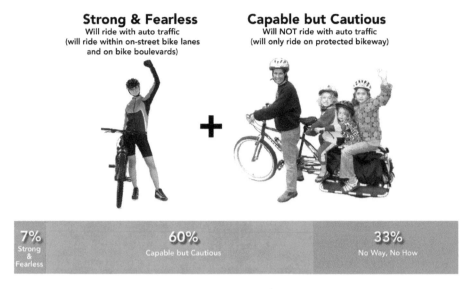

Strong & Fearless
Will ride with auto traffic
(will ride within on-street bike lanes
and on bike boulevards)

Capable but Cautious
Will NOT ride with auto traffic
(will only ride on protected bikeway)

7% Strong & Fearless	60% Capable but Cautious	33% No Way, No How

Potential Bike Riders

Surveys indicate that potential bicycle riders fall into three categories:

- *Strong and Fearless:* 7% of the population are confident riding their bicycles in bicycle lanes, or in the street along with other traffic.
- *Capable but Cautious:* 60% of the population would ride a bicycle, if they felt it was safe.
- *Remaining Citizens:* 33% of the population will never ride a bicycle.

The challenge is to create a bicycle system that feels safe enough to encourage the capable but cautious to bike. Unfortunately, lanes painted onto the street pavement aren't considered sufficiently safe by most people. Research indicates that these riders want a physical separation between their bicycles and the moving traffic.

The following considerations are paramount in locating a protected bikeway system through existing neighborhoods:

- Is there enough space available for the bikeway, or will it be necessary to take out a lane of traffic?
- Can funding be found to retrofit existing roadways to accommodate protected bikeways?

Unless the benefits of the system are developed in terms that individuals can relate to—increased disposable income, healthier bodies, improved net worth, and a reduction in greenhouse gas—there is little chance that a protected bikeway system will find community support.

Transit Options

The process for creating a good, or even great, transit system will vary according to the size of a city. Smaller cities may only be able to afford a bus system, whereas larger communities may be able to afford HCT systems, such as LRT, BRT, or streetcars.

Developers interested in offering proximity to transit as an amenity to buyers and renters prefer locations next to HCT. The HCT alignment and station locations are permanent, whereas bus stops are not. Stops disappear when bus routes are changed.

Whatever type of transit system is introduced into a community, transit stations should always be located in the center of a hub—not along neighborhood edges.

Economic Benefits

The potential benefits of neighborhood districts include both the reduction of greenhouse gas emissions by up to 50% and an economic stimulus for the local marketplace that results from money spent at local businesses rather than on gasoline.

Neighborhood district models have the potential to:

- reduce and shorten automobile trips significantly
- increase transit ridership
- provide a substantial local economic stimulus

BUILDING BLOCKS

Neighborhood districts are the basic building blocks for creating a Transformation Strategy.

The Transformation Strategy utilizes the neighborhood district planning models to improve the quality of life in the city and effectively address climate change.

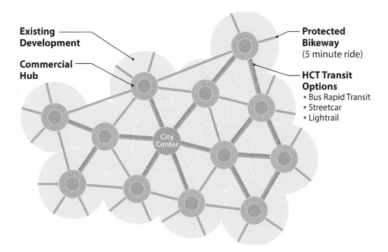

Neighborhood Districts Applied to City

The Transformation Strategy process works for cities of all sizes. A small city might consist of a single neighborhood district. Larger cities may have many neighborhood districts connected to each other and to the city center by transit and protected bikeway networks. The city center could be considered a neighborhood district with an employment emphasis.

Significant reductions in greenhouse gas emissions will require land use and transportation plans and policies that (1) reduce automobile use, and (2) limit sprawl. Neighborhood districts have the potential to do both. A city that adopts the neighborhood district planning model to guide land use and transportation policies will be well-positioned to adapt to a changing world.

Limiting Sprawl

Most cities accommodate growth by expanding outward. Commonly called "sprawl," this model creates low-density suburban development and stimulates automobile travel.

The alternative to expanding outward is to expand upward by increasing residential densities within the existing city boundaries. The neighborhood district provides a blueprint for how to accomplish the task.

In many cities the typical residential population density is approximately eight to ten units per acre. At that level of density, the population within a one-mile radius would be about 20,000 people.

In a neighborhood district, the density within a quarter-mile radius of a neighborhood center could increase over time to approximately sixty units per acre, resulting in an additional 9,000 people. Outside the quarter-mile radius, population density would be expected to change very little.

When the transition to a neighborhood district is completed, the population will have grown by 45%—from 20,000 to 29,000 people.

Reducing Automobile Use

A Transformation Strategy has the potential to reduce vehicle-miles traveled by up to 50%, in the following ways:

- *Shortening automobile trips:* Many of the goods and services needed by residents on a daily basis would be conveniently located in a mixed-use neighborhood center.

- *Eliminating automobile trips:* Protected bikeways and transit would connect residential areas to a mixed-use neighborhood hub, and to other neighborhood districts.

Regional Benefits

When the MOD model is applied to a regional transit system, the potential economic benefits can be substantial. The increased population density and convenient access to the area's transit stations translates into increased transit ridership and revenues from fares. And creating shorter and fewer automobile trips translates into a substantial green dividend.

My firm applied the MOD model to Edmonton's sixty-station LRT transit system, and estimated the anticipated green dividend and increased revenues from fares. While the results from a single-station area MOD were not necessarily impressive, the economic benefits from implementing MODs throughout the entire system were compelling.

If the MOD model were implemented at all stations, the potential to increase annual revenues from fares would rise from $2 million to $37 million. The anticipated economic stimulus "green dividend" with MOD was estimated at $127 million—without MOD, it was a meager $3 million.

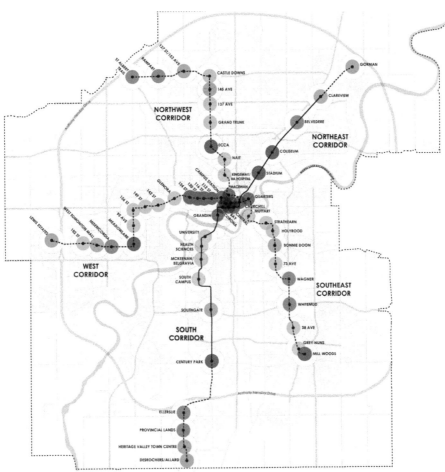

Economic Benefits (Annual)	Station Areas	
	Without MOD	With MOD
Transit Ridership	1 million trips	19 million trips
Farebox Revenue	$2 million	$37 million
Green Dividend	$3 million	$127 million

Edmonton: Benefits with and without MOD

CHAPTER THREE

Public Support

The public will always do the right thing if given good information and the opportunity to influence decision makers. The assumption that a massive public involvement process will provide superior results may not hold up. More does not necessarily mean better.

When my consulting firm was working in Santa Fe, a member of the City Council felt that we weren't doing enough to involve the public in the planning process. She believed that people who attended downtown public information meetings were more likely to support improvements to the downtown than suburban dwellers. She was convinced that suburbanites think differently and would reject the improvements we were proposing. She insisted we make the same presentation we were about to make downtown at a suburban community center on the following Saturday morning.

Approximately 150 people attended the downtown evening meeting. We presented twenty-three concepts that responded to the issues and concerns the public had identified in previous meetings. As is our custom, we provided ballots so that attendees could make their preferences known by checking either a yes, no, or other box. All twenty-three concepts were listed on the ballot.

At the end of our presentation we asked for comments and questions from the audience. At that point, a few individuals with issues unrelated to the planning process attempted to usurp the meeting. One particularly unruly young woman, shouting her concerns, was escorted from the meeting by security personnel. Other members of the audience helped calm the disruptive individuals, and we spent the remainder of the meeting answering questions.

Afterwards, the city councilor asked me, "Did anyone like anything?" I had already thumbed through the ballots and knew that most of the concepts had received a 90% or better yes vote. In the interest of not wanting to bias the Saturday morning vote by reporting the early downtown returns, I decided to keep the results confidential.

The Saturday morning public turnout was similar to the downtown meeting. The downtown meeting participants had been mostly businesspeople. The suburban turnout was mostly homeowners and renters. We made the same presentation and handed out the same ballots. The suburban audience was polite and thoughtful—a welcome change from the downtown evening session.

After the meeting ended, we compared the voting preferences from the two meetings. The urban and suburban votes were almost identical! This result was not surprising. Whenever we hold parallel public involvement programs to reach different income and cultural groups, whether using mail-in ballots or voting at the meeting, the results are the same.

Implementation Rules
Policies, Regulations, and Design Guidelines

Framework Plan
Retail, Employment, Housing, Civic Uses, Open Space, Complete Streets, Implementation

Public Support

Transformation Strategy Basic Elements

GETTING STARTED

Strong public support for any proposed urban improvement project is the foundation on which the entire planning process rests. Without a strong base of community supporters, even the best interventions risk never being implemented.

A Precious Commodity

Public involvement is a precious commodity that should never be wasted. It is important to recognize that the public has a limited attention span, and an extended or complicated public involvement process could jeopardize transformation efforts and discourage public participation. The public will respect a process that is efficient and inclusive.

If given good information, the public will always do the right thing. The challenge lies in making complex issues easily understood by nonprofessionals so that the public will take ownership of the final Transformation Strategy. Facilitating public contribution to the process requires skill and sensitivity.

Essential Players

The first step in putting together an effective process for public involvement is to establish a Steering Committee (SC) and a Technical Advisory Committee (TAC).

A typical steering committee includes representatives from various community interest groups, such as business, labor, retail, housing, culture, and neighborhoods. The committee has responsibility for reviewing the progress of the project and advising the hired consultants on issues that need to be addressed. Committee membership can be as few as a half-dozen people or as many as two to three dozen people.

A technical advisory committee should be composed of representatives from the public agencies that have jurisdiction and responsibilities in the area under study. Typical TAC membership may include individuals from the transportation, water, sewer, housing, planning, and development service bureaus.

Responsibilities of the TAC include reviewing project proposals and advising the consultant team on related technical issues.

Surprisingly, decision-makers—City Council members, for example—are often overlooked during the planning process. However, if they are left out of the process, the adoption of a Transformation Strategy and the support for plan implementation may be compromised. Decision-makers should be briefed periodically so that their questions can be answered and their suggestions incorporated into the planning process. It is vital to the overall success of the planning effort that decision-makers have their "fingerprints" on every completed Transformation Strategy.

Likewise, if the public is not enthusiastic about a Transformation Strategy, it will not be implemented. The essential challenge is to conduct a public involvement program that will generate support from the wider public, from invested agencies, and from public officials and important decision-makers.

INVOLVING THE PUBLIC

A national industry has grown up around the creation and administration of public involvement programs. Public involvement specialists provide an array of sophisticated services designed to elicit and sustain support for projects that impact large numbers of citizens. Unfortunately, watching some of these specialists in action leaves the impression that the issues that need to be addressed are secondary to the task of preventing the public from causing problems for decision-makers. On far too many projects, public participation has come to equal public manipulation. Like beer with fewer calories, the quality of the information that public involvement specialists often provide could be labeled "lite." Frequently, substantive or potentially controversial issues are avoided, and the goal becomes making the public feel good rather than incorporating their concerns in a meaningful way into the planning process.

Open House

A common form of "lite" public involvement is the open house. It typically entails inviting the public to a meeting at which information is displayed on tables and walls. People are free to walk around, read the information, and, if they have questions, talk to members of the planning team. The public's questions and comments are recorded by the planning team on flip charts, or directly onto the drawings on display.

The open-house format is problematic because the public is generally unfamiliar with the subject matter. In the absence of a carefully crafted presentation to educate the public about the issues, the public's ability to respond is limited. Also, most citizens are not accustomed to reading plans and deciphering information from drawings and sketches. Most importantly, there's always a risk that the public's questions and comments are susceptible to multiple interpretations, and may be construed by the design team in ways that suit their purposes.

Charrette

Another involvement technique for public participation is the charrette. A charrette involves a series of meetings usually held during the day. The goal is to get stakeholders and public activists in one place to discuss the project under consideration in order to develop consensus about potential design solutions.

The charrette format is not without its advantages but tends to work best with a small group of experts who have specialized knowledge the design team needs for its work, rather than with the public at large. As an example, if an academic campus or a medical facility is under design, educators and doctors may have special needs and requirements that the design team needs to understand. The charrette format provides an ideal opportunity for the design team to learn about the client's special needs. However, when charrettes are used with the general public, the design team may receive little usable information and the public's time may be wasted.

Consider the following factors when organizing the charrette:

- Consultants with drawing skills are needed to sketch design solutions suggested by the public.

- The multi-day format is often not practical for the working public.

- People who are not able or willing to attend a charrette due to scheduling conflicts still deserve an opportunity to participate in the process, even if in an abbreviated format.

- Key stakeholders may not be willing to participate in a charrette because they prefer to discuss their ideas with the design team in a confidential setting.

- Charrettes are expensive.

Unfortunately, charrettes have become a refuge for city planners and urban designers, especially those who lack competency in their respective fields. To compensate for shortcomings, some planners choose to rely on public input, which is seldom informed by the intricacies of urban design. All ideas and suggestions are "thrown at the wall," so to speak, to see what might stick. This approach is fun for participants but the outcome usually lacks substance. Charrettes, like open houses, provide "lite" design solutions.

Websites

Public agencies use websites to make planning documents available to the public and to provide information about upcoming meetings. Websites have limited effectiveness as a public involvement tool unless planning proposals are accompanied by:

- information to educate the public about why proposals are being considered

- feedback materials for quantifying the public's response to planning proposals

- staff to prepare materials and maintain the website

The limited public response to online information and the expense associated with preparing educational information and feedback materials should be factored in when considering how best to use the web.

Visioning

Visioning is an exercise in which planners ask members of the public to express their dreams and concerns. However, unless there is a clear understanding about how the acquired information will be used and integrated into the planning process, visioning exercises can be a waste of time and money.

Visioning is popular with many planners because most people enjoy it and therefore are enthusiastic about attending visioning sessions. People generally want to put forth their ideas, aspirations, and desires for the towns and cities they inhabit. But most of the resulting vision statements tend to be similar, and are often interchangeable. Though people everywhere like to think their particular city or town is unique, most people, I've found, share similar values and aspirations for the future, irrespective of where they happen to live.

The typical outcome of a visioning exercise is a series of goals and policies that address key issues identified during the process. As worthy as this may be, it is only a first step in the overall planning process. Unless a sound Framework Plan and a comprehensive set of Implementation Rules are also prepared, the vision will lead nowhere. Visioning exercises may be strung out over a period of many months or even years.

The question needs to be asked: is this prolonged, expensive visioning process really necessary? One answer can be found by taking a look at what happened in Portland, Oregon, over a period of twenty years.

Portland's Love Affair with Visioning

Portland's experience with engaging the public in visioning exercises over the years provides a useful lesson for other communities that may be attracted to the perceived benefits of visioning.

Clearly, Portland loves the visioning process! In twenty-four years the city produced five visions under four mayors for a cost of many millions of dollars. The only difference among the five visions was in the level of public outreach and the numbers of people involved. In every case, the visioning process tilled much of the same ground, and the issues and findings were remarkably similar.

Nobody would argue that any single aspiration that is the culmination of a visioning process is a bad thing in itself. Each and every idea is a worthy goal. But the bigger, more important question never got asked: was spending millions of public dollars the most expedient way to identify the generalized "apple-pie-and-motherhood" policies that resulted from them? The answer is simply *no*. The multiple visions are an indication of a dysfunctional planning profession.

It was in conjunction with the 1988 plan that Portland first began using the visioning technique. The city's previous plan, from 1972, had been produced without a public visioning process, and was regarded as highly successful. Nonetheless, the assumption was that with a visioning process, the next plan would be even better.

1988: Central City Plan – Vision 1

A public relations consultant was hired to promote the public outreach, theming it "Give Us Your Dreams." Everyone in Portland was invited to respond, including children. At the beginning of the process, a staff member from the city's Planning Bureau came by my office to talk about the visioning process. I asked how information was going to be collected, collated, and used. My visitor stared at me blankly and said, "We're only going to ask for people's dreams for the city." And that, unfortunately, is exactly what happened.

The Planning Bureau received over 10,000 responses. Among the more colorful suggestions was an idea to run cable cars from the tops of tall downtown buildings to the waterfront, something a group of children had come up with. Other science-fiction scenarios were worthy of a *Star Wars* episode. But once reality took hold, the question I had posed to my Planning Bureau visitor quickly emerged: what do we do with all this information, and how do we organize it? A good-faith effort was undertaken to categorize all the ideas and information that had flooded in, but after hundreds of hours of work, the many dreams and ideas for Portland's future turned out to be of very little use.

1991: Portland Future Focus – Vision 2

Not long after, in 1989, Mayor Bud Clark launched another visioning process, this time known as "Portland Future Focus." It employed a somewhat different methodology. The mayor and his staff handpicked fifty-five community leaders to research trends and then create a future vision for the city. Various techniques were used to involve the public, including a survey of community values, a speaker's bureau, a series of major policy meetings, open working-group meetings, and a newsletter. Policies were developed for each of the following sectors: crime, diversity, the economy, education, growth management, and leadership.

The final product, called a Strategic Plan, was completed in 1991. The effort involved more than 25,000 hours of volunteer time. It was a policy document without a single drawing or plan relating to Portland.

1999: Central Portland's Twenty-Five-Year Vision – Vision 3

Vera Katz followed Bud Clark as mayor. She initiated another ambitious visioning process: "Central Portland's Twenty-Five-Year Vision." The results of that visioning exercise are summarized under five main headings:

- America's Best Schools
- A Healthy River that Centers Our Community
- Complete Neighborhoods
- A Prosperous Region of Creativity and Imagination
- An Urban Environment that Defines Livability

2007: 2030 Vision – Vision 4

Six years on, yet another mayor, Tom Potter, launched his version of the visioning process. Potter's project lasted thirty-one months and entailed three phases. The first phase—the planning phase—took nine months to complete. The engagement phase lasted fifteen months; and the final phase, the analysis phase, was completed over a period of seven months. The budget for this huge undertaking was over $1.5 million, though insiders say the true cost may have been double that amount. City agencies received at least 13,000 response sheets from the public, at an average cost of $115 per response. The final report, published in 2009, organizes the vision statement under another set of five headings:

- Built Portland
- Economic Portland
- Environmental Portland

- Learning Portland
- Social Portland

City staff, together with the help of more than 380 people and organizations, produced the final document. The hefty report garnered national attention when it won the American Planning Association (APA) award in 2009.

2012: The Portland Plan – Vision 5

In 2009, another mayor, Sam Adams, announced his preparations for a strategic plan that would focus on the next twenty-five years of Portland's growth. The Portland Plan, as it was officially known, was adopted in 2012, and was the result of more than two years of research, dozens of workshops and informational fairs, hundreds of meetings with community groups, and more than 20,000 comments from local residents, businesses, and nonprofit organizations.

The stated intent of The Portland Plan was to identify and set policies and strategies in three main areas:

- thriving, educated youth
- facilities and programs that meet twenty-first century challenges and opportunities
- a healthy, connected city

Recent Plans

In 2016, after five years of work, Portland adopted the 2035 Comprehensive Plan. It is a long-range land use and public facility investment plan to guide future growth and physical development of the city.

EFFECTIVE PUBLIC INVOLVEMENT

Over the years, when I've prepared Transformation Strategies for my clients, I have found that the most efficient and cost-effective way to engage the public is through the use of informational workshops.

Information Workshops

There are two kinds of information workshops—the short and the long workshop. Both can be used to inform the public about the planning process and to receive their comments and suggestions.

Short Information Workshop

This workshop lasts one hour. It works well with small special-interest groups and elected officials. The workshop starts with a round of introductions and a 10-to-15-minute PowerPoint presentation summarizing project objectives and the planning process. Response sheets are handed out to everyone attending the workshop, and the remaining time is used to answer questions, receive comments, and fill out the response sheet.

The last ten minutes of the meeting are often the most revealing and valuable to the planning team. I ask each attendee to provide a final observation or comment, though they can pass if they wish. If we're seated around a table, I start the process by pointing to the individual next to me, then the next individual, and so on until I have acknowledged everyone around the table. This simple process gives those individuals who are reluctant to speak a space to be heard. What I have found is that those who have been silent throughout the meeting often provide the most valuable comments and insight.

Long Information Workshop

Long Information Workshop

This workshop lasts two to three hours depending on the size of the audience, which may range from 50 to 500 people. Tables accommodating up to ten people are used to display maps, drawings, and meeting materials. It is also important to have a large projection screen and a high-resolution projector, so that everyone in the room can see the screen.

A useful schedule for a long workshop begins with a half hour PowerPoint presentation that educates the public about the issues and possible solutions. Afterwards, fifteen minutes should be reserved for questions from the audience. So that all members of the audience are able to hear the questions, a wireless microphone should be available for each questioner.

After the questions, the next thirty minutes can be used for discussion of the presentation materials, filling out one-page response sheets, and designating someone at each table to give a short verbal report to the assembled audience, summarizing what was discussed at the table. The time required to complete this last step, the table reports, depends on the number of people in attendance.

Workshop Timing

Ideally, information workshops are held during each of the three major phases of the Framework Plan.

1. *At the onset of the Start Phase.* The public's issues and concerns are identified in this workshop and will become the reference point for creating urban design alternatives.

2. *During the Design Phase.* Once the urban design alternatives have been developed, they are presented to the public for their evaluation and preferences in one or two workshops.

3. *During the Implementation Phase.* Additional workshops can take place when various implementation strategies are under consideration.

In every workshop it is important to remind the public about the issues that they identified at the beginning of the planning process and how the evolving plan and alternatives respond to those issues.

The practice of holding public information workshops is uncomplicated and efficient. Concerned people can usually find the time to attend at least a few workshops.

If a problem is complex and the public does not understand the implications of any given proposal, the natural reaction will be skepticism and opposition. The challenge is to take adequate time to prepare easy-to-understand materials that are clearly linked to the interests and concerns initially identified by the public.

It is vitally important that at all information meetings, attendees are invited to fill out a one-page response sheet, or ballot, at the conclusion of each session so that they have the opportunity to indicate their preferences for the various alternatives under consideration.

Ballots

I have found that what is voiced during a public meeting is seldom representative of what the larger public audience is thinking. The verbal exchanges that take place in public meetings are nearly always misleading and give little indication of the public's true feelings. More often than not, those opposed to a project are quick to let everyone know why they are opposed, while those in favor remain generally silent. A ballot is the best way to measure public opinion accurately, and voting is the only trustworthy means for determining where the public stands with regard to specific schemes for achieving established goals.

In order for the vote to be successful and provide an accurate record of public sentiment, the following components must be in place:

- clear, accurate educational materials
- high-quality graphics illustrating alternative scenarios
- a simple ballot offering voters the opportunity to respond with a *yes, no,* or *other*

Ballots make many planners uncomfortable, because the results may turn out to be contrary to the planner's agenda and derail a preferred course of action. The safer approach, from a planner's perspective, would be to ask open-ended, generalized questions, thereby leaving plenty of room for interpreting the results more freely, and concluding that the public agrees with the planner's conclusions.

Personally, I have never seen a city plan succeed without the broad, informed support of its community. Unless the public understands the proposals that are set forth in the plan and has had a hand in weighing the merits of alternative proposals, even the best city plan will inevitably go awry. The ballot box provides the best method for building community support.

The Case for the Ballot

In my career as an urban design consultant, I have found that the ballot is the single best tool for incorporating the public's preferences into an effective Transformation Strategy. My experience working with the city of Missoula, Montana clearly demonstrates the power of the ballot.

As part of our efforts to revitalize downtown Missoula, we had proposed constructing a system of protected bikeways using the Mobility-Oriented District (MOD) planning model. The majority of residents were in favor of the concept.

Local biking groups, on the other hand, didn't want protected bikeways because they preferred the full freedom of the roadways. The biking enthusiasts would brook no interference with their "right to roam"—even if it meant saving lives and promoting more bicycling. A representative of these biking groups sat on both the steering committee and the technical advisory committee for the planning effort, and would have killed our proposal if we had not been able to produce hard evidence that the vast majority of Missoulians were in favor of the idea. Fortunately, we had given citizens the vote and the ballots showed that 95% of the public favored protected bikeways. Two years later, I'm pleased to say, Missoula inaugurated its first phase of downtown transformation by building protected bikeways along its historic downtown shopping street.

The ballot can be used to determine the public's position on a whole array of issues that impact transformation efforts. For example, a public plaza may be under consideration on a particular site and local residents are given the vote. If a solid majority is in favor of the proposed location, you can move forward with the scheme with confidence. If it is a split vote, or very nearly split, you know that the concept needs to be discarded or altered. And if there is less than a 50% positive vote, drop the project altogether.

There are other benefits to having a ballot. When a consensus is lacking on how to deal with an urban design issue, there is always the potential that a vocal minority may become disruptive if their position is not embraced. But with ballot results in hand, it is harder to contest the preferences of a solid majority. Minority dissenters will quickly recognize this and concede the issue.

The public should be skeptical of any public involvement exercise that does not include a ballot. Without a vote, planners can manipulate the urban transformation process to fit their own preferences or preconceptions. Ballots ensure that the public's wishes are valued and respected.

Typical Ballot

The tally from a typical meeting illustrates how the ballot identifies proposals for which there is substantial support, and those that may need more work.

For the sake of simplicity, it is recommended that ballot questions be limited to the most important issues facing the city, and that responses are limited to a simple *yes*, *no*, or *other*—along with an opportunity to elaborate on any concerns that may require more commentary.

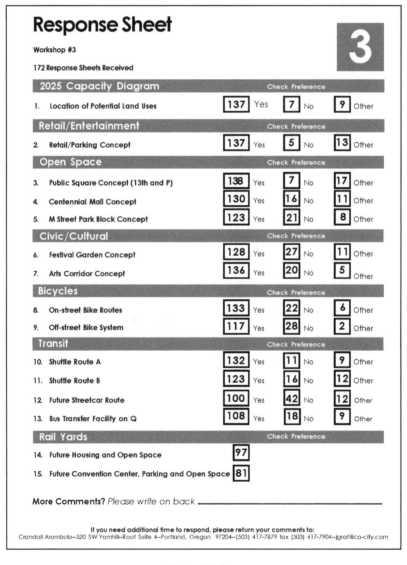

Response Sheet

Workshop #3

172 Response Sheets Received

3

2025 Capacity Diagram		Check Preference				
1. Location of Potential Land Uses	137 Yes	7 No	9 Other

Retail/Entertainment		Check Preference			
2. Retail/Parking Concept	137 Yes	5 No	13 Other

Open Space		Check Preference			
3. Public Square Concept (13th and P)	138 Yes	7 No	17 Other
4. Centennial Mall Concept	130 Yes	16 No	11 Other
5. M Street Park Block Concept	123 Yes	21 No	8 Other

Civic/Cultural		Check Preference			
6. Festival Garden Concept	128 Yes	27 No	11 Other
7. Arts Corridor Concept	136 Yes	20 No	5 Other

Bicycles		Check Preference			
8. On-street Bike Routes	133 Yes	22 No	6 Other
9. Off-street Bike System	117 Yes	28 No	2 Other

Transit		Check Preference			
10. Shuttle Route A	132 Yes	11 No	9 Other
11. Shuttle Route B	123 Yes	16 No	12 Other
12. Future Streetcar Route	100 Yes	42 No	12 Other
13. Bus Transfer Facility on Q	108 Yes	18 No	9 Other

Rail Yards		Check Preference
14. Future Housing and Open Space	97	
15. Future Convention Center, Parking and Open Space	81	

More Comments? *Please write on back* _____

If you need additional time to respond, please return your comments to:
Crandall Arambula--520 SW Yamhill--Roof Suite 4--Portland, Oregon 97204--(503) 417-7879 fax (503) 417-7904--jgraf@ca-city.com

Typical Ballot

Representative Opinion Sampling

People often wonder about the number of respondents it takes to obtain a representative sampling. I have found again and again in my work that people who take the time to attend a public involvement workshop usually provide a reliable snapshot of how the larger community feels. Below are two examples:

- For *Milwaukie, Oregon* we prepared a Transformation Strategy incorporating our standard process for public involvement workshops and the use of ballots. But Milwaukie city administrators felt that our sampling was too limited. They asked us to mail the information we had presented in public meetings to every household in the city, with an accompanying mail-in ballot. Approximately 7,000 households received our materials, and over 15% of them returned the ballot—a rate of return considered high by professional pollsters, who generally expect no more than a 3% return rate. In the end, the results from the mail-in vote were identical to those we had received at the public meetings.

- In *Santa Fe* we found results obtained from the public, from special-interest groups, and from stakeholders in a limited number of downtown public workshops were exactly the same as those from a suburban community.

Statisticians may argue that the small percentage of the population who get involved in a transformation process is not a statistically significant indicator of the public's preferences. However true that may be, it can also be said that the public has been well-informed of meetings and agendas through an extensive advertising campaign. All residents are given the opportunity to attend meetings, but it is the most concerned and opinionated members of the public who will make the effort to participate.

The turnout for a large public meeting will vary, depending on the size of the community and the local interest in transformation. In Lincoln, Nebraska, for example, meetings were held in the convention center, with attendance by well over 300 people. In Fairbanks, Alaska, meetings were held in hotel ballrooms and a hockey arena, and attendance was in the hundreds. In Missoula, Montana, meetings were held in a hotel ballroom and attracted approximately 250 people.

Public Outreach Budget

The amount of money allocated to a public outreach effort should be limited to no more than 15–20% of the total budget for a Transformation Strategy.

Public involvement is most cost-effective when the public is:

- educated about what works and what does not
- provided with site-specific physical design alternatives illustrating different ways to respond to project goals
- provided with an evaluation of how well the individual alternatives respond to the project goals
- invited to identify their preferences by ballot

A small sampling of public opinion can be a very accurate indicator of overall public sentiment. It is the quality, not the quantity, of the public involvement program that makes the difference.

ONGOING INVOLVEMENT

The momentum needed to implement a Transformation Strategy should be well underway within the first few years of a plan's completion. Because government staff and other agency employees rarely have the political clout or connections to generate that kind of momentum, an implementation committee should be assembled to oversee and guarantee implementation. Membership of the implementation committee should include, ideally, a mix of elected officials and local business and civic leaders. Without an implementation committee, or some form of ongoing public advocacy group, plans wither and end up on the shelf.

Over time the composition of a City Council will surely change. Members will come and go depending on elections or job turnover. Public employees also come and go. Those who were involved in developing a Transformation Strategy may be reassigned or change jobs. Only an implementation committee will be able to provide the continuity so essential for putting the strategy into action and overseeing implementation. It is best if members of an implementation committee serve for at least five years.

The following stories from cities where I have worked underscore how important it is to have an implementation committee of sufficient size:

- In *Knoxville, Tennessee,* a talented and energetic group of people calling themselves Nine Counties One Vision initiated the city's transformation efforts. As its name implies, the group represented a constituency larger than the downtown. Once the final transformation plan had been completed and this well-connected group of citizens disbanded there was no longer a powerful group of people available to provide ongoing advocacy for implementation of the plan. Consequently, Knoxville's transformation efforts were severely compromised.

- In *Santa Fe, New Mexico,* the implementation committee was comprised of only six members, most of whom were political appointees whose interests lay more with the City Council than with the concerns of the public. Ultimately, this small group had little staying power and lacked the mandate to focus on implementation. In short, there was no effective advocacy for implementing the recommendations of Santa Fe's plan, and the city suffered accordingly.

- The story was slightly different in *Racine, Wisconsin.* The client for the Transformation Strategy was a public advocacy committee. The committee was comprised of representatives from several downtown interest groups, and it stayed involved throughout the duration of the planning process. From start to finish, the committee provided oversight and continuity. After five years, the majority of the strategy recommendations had been implemented. Indeed, the strategy was such a success that a second downtown plan was commissioned—this time for a much larger area of the city, and with the same committee serving as the client.

- *Whitefish, Montana,* with a population of 7,500 people, had three mayors, two city managers, two planning directors, and a big turnover of seats on the City Council over a period of eight years. The constant was an existing organization called "Heart of Whitefish," a group representing downtown business interests. This organization provided the institutional memory needed to implement the downtown master plan that was completed in 2005. This highly effective group of citizens monitored all the implementation activities, and when a proposal turned out to degrade rather than improve the downtown, they were quick to inform elected officials and make suggestions as to how to correct the situation. Most of the recommendations in the 2005 plan as well as those from an updated 2013 plan were implemented.

- When I became involved with *Missoula, Montana* in 2009, this city of 67,000 was well ahead of the game. They had several organizations already in place that were capable of managing the downtown's Transformation Strategy: a downtown business improvement district (BID), the Missoula Redevelopment Agency (MRA), and the Missoula Downtown Association (MDA). These groups banded together with other organizations to form the Downtown Master Plan Implementation Team. Other members of the team included the city's Transportation Plan Manager, the Plan Services Manager, the Housing Authority, the Parking Commission, the transit agency, a City Council member, and a downtown businessman.

In a 2013 report to the Missoula City Council, the implementation team summarized its purpose as follows:

- to meet monthly
- to keep the Transformation Strategy alive and breathing
- to tackle topics and components of the Transformation Strategy, set goals, and seek community members to serve on committees in order to engage with, advocate for, and achieve goals
- to oversee the plan through completion
- to recognize that citywide support is essential in order to implement the plan
- to acknowledge that the accomplishments of the Transformation Strategy are the result of a community-wide effort

In the group's annual report to the City Council, it provided:

- an update of accomplishments from the previous year
- a list of all accomplishments of the Transformation Strategy since its inception
- a summary of immediate goals for the near future

Missoula's success in implementing its Transformation Strategy was due to the commitment and ongoing efforts of its solid, highly inclusive advocacy group. Missoula's implementation team provides an ideal, universal model for communities everywhere that are interested in turning a Transformation Strategy into action, and keeping it off the shelf.

The rule of thumb for successful implementation is that when an advocacy group, or implementation committee, is involved from the beginning of a transformation effort and remains engaged for three to five years after the Transformation Strategy is completed, the strategy has a very high rate of success.

CHAPTER FOUR

Framework Plan

The design criteria for creating successful neighborhoods, plazas, streets, and retail are very specific. Solutions for fixing a city can be developed only by using fundamental urban design criteria to prepare and evaluate site-specific designs.

In the 1990s, fifty years after Frank Lloyd Wright had completed his seminal SC Johnson Administration Building in Racine, Wisconsin, the historic downtown was suffering. Like many Rust Belt cities, Racine was experiencing an economic decline and urban decay due to the shrinking of its once-powerful industrial sector.

City business leaders, looking for a way to reverse this downward trend, had commissioned an expensive market study to help them identify key businesses and retailers that could be attracted to a community like Racine. The findings were predictable and not very encouraging. Because Racine is a lakefront city, half of what would typically be considered the market area was actually water. One economist quipped, "And the fish aren't buying anything!"

Nonetheless, wanting to move forward with the goal of rejuvenating Racine, the SC Johnson Foundation invited me to make a presentation about the city's prospects to a group of business leaders and elected officials. I explained to them how a Transformation Strategy could turn things around. They were intrigued, but also had concerns about how they could justify the money already spent on the market study. I suggested they refer to the market study as Phase One, and the Transformation Strategy as Phase Two. That simple solution worked.

One year on, Racine's Transformation Strategy was complete and had been adopted in a unanimous vote by the City Council. Five years after that, nearly all of the strategy's recommendations had been implemented.

A major component of Racine's strategy was a series of public improvements, or game changers, that were designed to stimulate private investment. The first game changer was the construction of a string of park blocks that connected the heart of the downtown to the lake. These blocks provided adjacent development sites that were attractive to investors who had made it known that, if the park blocks were built, they would bring their business to the city. On that promise, Racine spent $3 million to construct the park blocks, and private developers immediately invested more than $50 million in new projects.

Some years later I was attending the groundbreaking ceremonies for a large housing project with substantial retail space on Racine's Main Street. Standing next to me was the out-of-town developer responsible for the project. I asked him why he had been attracted to Racine. His response: "This is the only city in Wisconsin that knows what it wants to be when it grows up."

Implementation Rules
Policies, Regulations, and Design Guidelines

Framework Plan
Retail, Employment, Housing, Civic Uses,
Open Space, Complete Streets,
Implementation

Public Support

Transformation Strategy Basic Elements

THE HEART OF THE TRANSFORMATION STRATEGY

The Framework Plan is the heart of a Transformation Strategy. If the Framework is weak, the Transformation Strategy will not succeed. It will become a shelf plan.

The development of a Framework Plan involves:

- preparing land use and transportation alternatives that are responsive to a community's unique issues and concerns
- using fundamental urban design principles to prepare alternative site-specific designs
- evaluating alternatives in terms of financial implications and ability to stimulate change
- selecting and refining preferred alternatives
- establishing an implementation strategy (priorities and schedule)

Fundamental Principles

Land use and circulation improvements need to be designed in accordance with fundamental urban design principles. At a minimum, a Framework Plan needs to include urban design solutions for:

- retail
- public plazas
- neighborhoods
- parks
- employment districts
- civic uses
- complete streets
- public transit

Implementation

The challenge is to produce a Framework Plan that creates significant momentum towards implementation. Immediate success can turn skeptics into believers. Momentum can be established by prioritizing five to ten projects that can be implemented within the first five years.

Game Changers and Silver Bullets

Game Changers are public projects that stimulate private investment. Silver Bullets are public and private projects that erode the city investment environment. A successful Framework Plan must include Game Changers. Plans that do not include Game Changers are difficult to implement. Silver Bullet projects should be avoided.

LAND USE FUNDAMENTALS

Determining appropriate land use is fundamental in designing the features of a city. For example, how best to configure the retail offerings in the downtown so that it thrives? How can parking be designed and located so that it is retail-friendly? Where should a public plaza be located so that it is an asset and not a liability? Where do public parks belong, and what features should they include to best serve neighborhoods? What does it take to attract and maintain employment opportunities in the central city? How can the city create residential neighborhoods with affordable housing and higher density?

Retail

A city center without healthy retail is not a place anyone wants to visit or spend time. Everything a shopper might need should be concentrated in a pedestrian-friendly retail environment located in the center of a city or a neighborhood.

In every city where I've worked as a consultant, the story has been the same. At one time the downtown had been a thriving retail center. Then big-box stores are built on large tracts of inexpensive land in the suburbs, decreasing the downtown share of the retail market. Retailers begin abandoning the downtown in favor of more profitable suburban locations. The pedestrian environment in the downtown deteriorates even more as vacant buildings are demolished to create surface parking lots. The combination of a diminished retail offering and a hostile pedestrian environment turns the downtown into a place shoppers want to avoid.

When a community starts considering downtown transformation, often the first course of action is to retain an economist to do a market survey. The thinking is that an economist will identify market trends and emerging niches for which retailers can be recruited. The problem is that economists tend to base their projections on past trends, and if past trends are negative, the projections will never be encouraging.

Retail Fundamentals

Retail Main Street

I prefer to believe that there will always be a potential for retail if conditions are right, and that retailers will be attracted to locations where risk is minimized and success is possible. The trick is to attract the retailer by designing a retail environment that has the potential to be more appealing than any other location in the city. I call this approach "inducing market demand."

Retail Configuration

Determining the right type of configuration for creating a successful retail environment is not mysterious. Whenever a retail developer wants to build a new retail street, shopping mall, or lifestyle center, he or she invariably uses a formula that hasn't changed in decades—the historic Main Street. The Main Street model, with its shops on the ground level along both sides of the street—shops that continue without interruption—is foolproof.

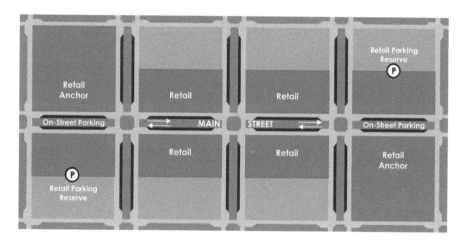

Historic Main Street

Typically, a grocery or department store serves as an anchor at either end of the street. The length of the street usually does not exceed 1,300 feet—or a comfortable five-minute walk—and curbside parking is readily available along both sides of the street.

Shoppers should be able to find everything they need on a successful Main Street. The amount of retail space required to accommodate a comprehensive mix of shops is approximately 150,000 square feet. At a minimum, an ideal configuration would include a grocery store, a drugstore, clothing stores, restaurants, and coffee shops.

No commercial uses, such as banks, drive-through services, exercise studios, or offices should interfere with the continuous row of street-level retail activities along the Main Street. There should be no blank walls and no building setbacks, and fast-food restaurants should not be permitted to sit back from the street in order to accommodate drive-throughs.

Attractive shop fronts are essential to creating a pleasant experience for shoppers. The shops lining the street should have large, well-lit windows, and all shop fronts should engage the pedestrian passing on the sidewalk.

Pedestrian Environment

A successful retail street is always designed with the pedestrian as the top priority—never the automobile. Sidewalks should be wide, with plenty of places to sit and rest or wait for a friend. There should also be adequate space on the sidewalks for landscaping, and for displaying artwork and shop merchandise. The minimum width of a pleasant sidewalk is twelve feet. Awnings and arcades, also essential elements of attractive sidewalks, help protect shoppers in rain, snow, or bright sunshine.

Pedestrian Crossings

Shoppers should never feel threatened by automobile traffic. Every intersection must feel safe and comfortable for pedestrian crossing. The distance to cross the street should be kept to a minimum by using curb extensions. Walk signals should be automatic, rather than incorporating push buttons, so that pedestrians don't have to ask permission to cross the street. Ideally, roadways at intersections are elevated six inches in order to eliminate curbs altogether, and allow pedestrians to traverse an intersection without having to step off or onto a curb.

Parking

Many downtown retailers and parking consultants don't understand what constitutes parking suitable to support retail activity. If parking is not adequate, shoppers will be reluctant to go downtown. Even if curb-side parking is available along the main and side streets, it typically provides less than half of the parking required for retail. Additional parking should be provided on the backside of the retail blocks or in parking structures connected to the primary retail street.

Automobile Access

Downtown shops should always be easy to find and convenient to access by automobile. Retail that is located in out-of-the-way places often fails.

Retail Parking

Office workers are not nearly as selective as shoppers and others heading to downtown for entertainment or a meal. When it comes to looking for a parking space, office workers are more likely to park in dark, dingy parking structures that are difficult to access, because nothing else is available. But retail shoppers will not.

Downtown retail has to compete with the ease of parking at suburban shopping malls, with their spacious "grandma-friendly" parking lots and structures. Shoppers will avoid the downtown if "grandma-friendly" parking is not available. The characteristics of good retail parking solutions are summarized below.

Retail Parking Structure Fundamentals

Disguised Retail Parking Structure

Location

A parking structure should be located no more than a half-block from the primary retail street or shopping destination. If a shopper has to cross a street to access the retail street, the parking will be perceived as being too far away.

Automobile Circulation

One-way circulation works best in parking structures because the driver never has to worry about running into an approaching car. It allows the driver to make continuous right-hand turns while searching for a parking space and leaving the structure. Simplicity and predictability are the most important criteria when it comes to circulation in a parking structure; dead ends are unacceptable.

Pedestrian Safety

Pedestrian safety is an important design consideration that is often overlooked. Pedestrians need to feel safe when making the journey from the parked car to the street, and should never be in a situation where they can't be seen. This means that parking structures must be well-lit and open to viewing from adjacent floors. Stairwells and elevators should be adjacent to the street, with plenty of windows that allow viewing from the street.

Ground Floor

Pedestrian-friendly streets require lively building facades at the street level, and parking structures should be no exception. Active uses on the ground floor, such as retail shops and other commercial enterprises, should have facades that are at least 75% transparent, providing views into the interior space from the sidewalk.

Street Corners

It is strongly recommended that the ground floor corners of parking structures contain retail and commercial storefronts so that intersections are active and enhance the pedestrian experience. Elevators and stairways should not be located on the corners of parking structures that face an intersection.

Character

The facades of utilitarian parking structures are often unpleasant and even ugly, degrading the urban environment. In urban settings, the facades of parking structures should be designed to be compatible with adjacent buildings. Indeed, the best facades do not look like parking structures at all.

The photograph on the previous page is a good example of a harmonious parking structure design located in downtown Portland, Oregon. A new eighteen-story building is adjacent to a ten-story historic building. The first ten floors of the new building are parking. The façade enclosing the parking uses a design vocabulary (color, window size and placement, detailing) similar to that found on the historic building.

Restaurants and a hotel lobby occupy the ground floor. As I often say to visitors to whom I'm giving a downtown tour, "You are standing in close proximity to the largest parking structure in downtown. Can you find it?" Some people think it must be below grade, while others, after looking around, just shrug. Invariably, no one is able to spot it.

Public Plaza

A community without a public plaza is like a home without a living room. The most memorable cities and towns in the world all have public plazas—magical places that bring life and economic vitality to their surroundings.

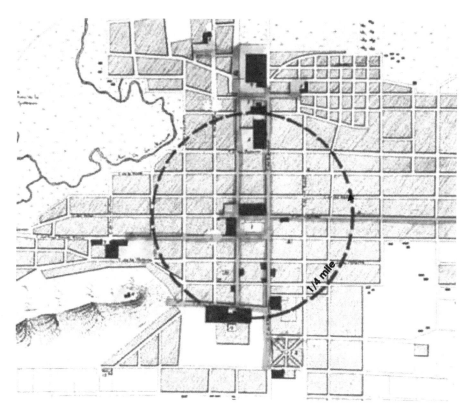

San Cristobal de las Casas

The concept of the public plaza came to the Americas from Europe. In 1573 King Phillip II of Spain signed the Laws of the Indies that codified the city planning process, prescribing a public plaza in every city in Spanish territory. Colonists used King Philip's 148 ordinances to locate and build their settlements in the new world. The plaza in San Cristobal de las Casas, in the highlands of southern Mexico, predates the Laws of the Indies but closely follows the prescribed formula. The 1520s plan illustrates the basic plaza concept. The plaza is situated in the center of a grid of streets running north and south, and east and west. Roads extend out from the plaza to smaller neighborhood plazas located a quarter of a mile, or a five-minute walk, away. On one side a church borders the plaza; on another, government buildings. Shops line the remaining two sides.

The layout of San Cristobal and its plaza is not unique. The plazas in Santa Fe, New Mexico, and in Albuquerque, New Mexico, are similar.

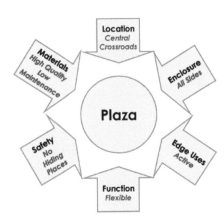

Plaza Fundamentals

Urban Plaza

Location

Though many communities would like to create a square or plaza as the focal point of their downtown transformation, few have the ability to do so. A good site can be difficult to find, and establishing the necessary conditions along the edge of the site to ensure the plaza's success is often just as challenging.

Because a plaza must be in the symbolic "heart" of a city, only a few sites in a city are suitable for building a new plaza. The heart of a city can be the center of a commercial district, the crossroads of a circulation system, or the historic city center. Wherever it is, the location must have the potential to provide enclosure, activities around the edges of the plaza, and sufficient size to accommodate large public gatherings.

Plazas that do not satisfy these basic requirements risk neglect, and may turn into undesirable backwaters. Backwater plazas may feel unsafe.

Enclosure

A plaza should be thought of as an enclosed open space, an outdoor "room." In order to be successful, it must have well-defined edges. The enclosure defines the space and provides a sense of intimacy. Often adjacent buildings provide enclosure. Other enclosing elements, such as columned arcades or landscaping, are sometimes used to good effect.

Edge Uses

The great plazas of the world are surrounded on all four sides by a variety of active ground-floor uses, such as restaurants, shops, markets, or hotels. Plazas bordered by inactive uses, such as banks and office, do not attract the foot traffic needed to become animated.

Function

A plaza should be designed to enable all kinds of public events, such as farmers markets, flower shows, lunch-hour performances, winter skating rinks, or summer concerts. It should be inviting to people of all ages and offer plenty of places to sit and enjoy an activity or visit with friends. Sometimes designers can become too enthusiastic, cluttering a plaza with design features that limit its ability to accommodate large gatherings. Clutter can be monuments, water features, children's play areas, performance stages, or landscaping in the wrong location.

A common mistake is to combine a plaza with a park. Usually, when this happens, both are compromised.

Safety

Plazas need to feel safe, both day and night. Any design feature that restricts sight lines into and through the space should be avoided. Lighting is vital so that pedestrians feel comfortable walking through the plaza in the late evening.

Materials

Because plazas are heavily used, they must be able to take a lot of wear and tear over time. All construction materials should, therefore, be of the highest quality, as well as low in maintenance.

Urban Parks

Parks and open spaces are essential quality-of-life amenities for urban areas. The function of an urban park is different from that of a plaza. Parks are designed with specific areas set aside for recreational activities or quiet contemplation. Grassy areas, trees, and pathways typically dominate. A plaza, on the other hand, consists of hardscape—a ground surface that is paved to accommodate large public gatherings throughout the year in all weather conditions.

Early city planners understood that parks are important additions to dense urban communities and provide much-needed open space, natural settings, and visual relief to the city, as well as space for public recreation.

Some communities—like Portland, Oregon, and Savannah, Georgia—were fortunate in that early city fathers created a system of park blocks within the city. These lovely green spaces make living and working downtown pleasant for residents, shoppers, and businesses.

Urban Park Fundamentals   Urban Park

Location

Ideally, urban parks should be located so that they provide easy access for people living in adjacent neighborhoods. In high-density residential neighborhoods, parks are even more essential. The best configuration is one in which every residential and employment neighborhood is within three blocks of an urban park.

Circulation

Circulation systems within a park will, in part, be determined by the size of the park and the types of recreational facilities it contains. A common error when designing an urban park is to force pedestrians to travel around the edges of the park in order to reach the other side. It is preferable to create pathways that pass through the park, thereby activating the space and channeling pedestrian movement through recreational facilities.

Character

Wherever possible, each park should have a unique character, and not merely be a replica of some other park. Character can be determined by considering the needs of the community or neighborhood where the park is located.

Function

Parks should be designed to accommodate a variety of functions. Neighborhood parks, for example, would benefit from having ample room for sports fields. Smaller parks are well-suited to children and could include fountains and accommodations for family picnics. Other types of parks are natural areas or urban wetlands. In every case, the park design should be responsive to the unique characteristics of the neighborhood.

Safety

Safety becomes an issue if an urban park contains places where people could hide. Security improves when all areas of a park can be viewed from the park perimeter. Adequate lighting will reduce nighttime problems and improve security. Park designs should always be reviewed with safety issues in mind.

Users

Urban parks should appeal to a wide variety of users and age groups. It is important that there is seating available for quiet contemplation or group discussions. There should also be places for strolling while enjoying the outdoors, and for children's play.

Urban Neighborhoods

The creation of high-density housing neighborhoods (more units per acre) in the city center is an essential ingredient in any transformation effort.

A vibrant neighborhood supports retail, restaurants, small businesses, and transit. If essential services are in close proximity, walking often becomes a substitute for an automobile trip; and when trips are made by car, they will generally be shorter. High-density housing also requires less energy for heating and cooling than does a typical single-family home.

Urban Neighborhood Fundamentals

Urban Neighborhood

Location

In urban areas, there are frequently opportunities for infill housing on vacant lots or on the upper floors of older buildings. While it is helpful to take advantage of these opportunities, they do not have the potential to increase the inventory of downtown housing to a significant degree. Underutilized land, such as abandoned industrial areas or old rail yards located within proximity of a downtown core, offer much better opportunities for providing new high-density neighborhoods.

Retail and Services

All neighborhoods need essential retail services, such as a grocery store and a drugstore. Other desirable neighborhood businesses include restaurants, clothing stores, shoe stores, barbers, and hair salons. When developing a new neighborhood, the location of retail shops should not be left to chance; designating the location and configuration of retail opportunities will enhance the potential for success of the new businesses.

Open Space

All urban neighborhoods need convenient access to open space. In high-density neighborhoods, a well-designed nearby open space is a quality-of-life essential.

Incomes

Urban neighborhoods should be designed to accommodate people from all income and age demographics. Condominiums, market-rate rentals, and affordable housing can and should coexist. At a minimum, 20% of all housing in an urban neighborhood should be affordable.

Portland, Oregon's Pearl District provides a good example of how affordable housing can be successfully integrated into a popular urban setting. Twenty-five blocks of new housing were completed around 2010 at approximately 100 units per acre. Five blocks are dedicated to affordable housing. The casual observer would not be able to identify from the outside which buildings contain affordable housing and which have market-rate rentals. They are all well-designed and constructed with durable materials.

Pedestrians and Bicycles

People are attracted to environments that provide safe walking and bicycling—connecting housing to shopping, open space, and employment. In order to be safe, a bicycle network needs to provide adequate separation from automobiles through the use of curbs or landscaping. Painting bicycle lanes onto the street pavement provides insufficient protection.

Schools

The proximity of quality schools is a big consideration for young families. Urban designers need to coordinate with educators to ensure that the educational expectations of families will be met.

Employment Districts

According to recent trends, job seekers prefer to work for employers in downtowns with plenty of shops, restaurants, and convenient transit. Employers with worksites located adjacent to amenities, entertainment, and cultural activities have a competitive hiring edge. Employment sites become even more attractive if rental properties and for-sale housing are in close proximity. Developers who are aware of this shift in desirability understand that the best investment opportunities for offices and the other buildings that employers seek are downtown, not in the suburbs.

Employment District Fundamentals

Office Employment District

Visibility

Developers of large office buildings prefer prominent sites. High building visibility is an opportunity for perpetual advertising.

Location

Every business prefers to have a prestige location, if possible. It could be an area where other large office buildings are located, or a site with special views. Or it could be adjacent to a prestigious park, plaza, or cultural facility.

Access

Proximity to transit is becoming a more important determinant for developers when selecting sites for constructing offices and related facilities. More employers are recognizing that a large percentage of their workers want to avoid an automobile commute, and prefer to have a job convenient to transit. Bicycle commuting is also growing rapidly. Many prospective employees seek an employment site connected to a well-defined bicycle network with protected bikeways. Many employers now realize that providing secure bicycle parking and showers for their employees offers an additional incentive for people to work for them.

Shopping and Services

The most desirable employment sites are those where employees can walk out the door to find a restaurant or café to have lunch. The least desirable are those where employees have to drive to restaurants and shops.

Pedestrian Environment

The quality of the pedestrian environment is important to many prospective employees. The availability of safe places to walk or even run at lunchtime may be a central factor in their employment decision.

Civic Uses

Civic and cultural uses include community centers, city halls, courthouses, government buildings, and performing arts centers.

It is very common for communities with a strong interest in the arts, to think that building a new cultural facility may be the way to jump-start an anemic local economy. However, with very few exceptions, a cultural facility will not be self-supporting at first, or even for many years to come. It can often take a considerable amount of time before a city or town has a population large enough to support a new cultural facility, or for the local government to be able to provide the financial subsidies required to keep the doors open. Therefore, as a rule of thumb, cultural facilities should not be among the top priorities when embarking on a city transformation effort.

Another challenge to get right is a convention center. As appealing as the idea of having a convention center may be, it is a very competitive business. Convention centers that are most attractive to event organizers have an adjacent headquarters hotel as well as restaurants and shopping within walking distance. Sites that have the potential to provide these fundamental requirements can be hard to find for a number of reasons. The large parcel of land necessary for constructing big exhibit halls may not be available within a central downtown area. Even if a site is available, the warehouse-like characteristics of a convention center do not necessarily make for a good neighbor to pre-existing activities and structures in the downtown. Another often-overlooked consideration is that if the facility is eventually successful, sufficient area in which to expand may not be available.

Civic Use Fundamentals

Urban Civic Use

Location

Civic and cultural facilities located in the city center add to the economic vitality of the downtown by attracting customers to retail and other services. The presence of government workers who frequent restaurants and shops contribute to the health of the downtown economy.

Government buildings grouped in close proximity to one another can provide one-stop services for the public. Conversely, automobile travel is encouraged when civic agencies and government buildings are scattered throughout the city.

Site

It is not enough to locate important government buildings, such as city halls and courthouses, in the city center. As symbols of government, they deserve to be located on prominent sites.

Access

Convenient access means a building is easy to find and parking is readily available. Venues for cultural events will suffer financially if convenient parking is not available within walking distance of the venue.

Proximity

People who attend cultural events often like to have dinner before or after an event. Having a cultural facility within walking distance of restaurants can help stimulate attendance at events and promote restaurant dining.

Character

Though cultural buildings can be noteworthy for their unique architectural expression, it is also important that they reflect a community's values. For example, if a building is inserted into a historic neighborhood, the new building should respond to its historical context and not appear out of place. As a gesture of respect, the building should use some elements of the established architectural vocabulary in order to fit in with its neighbors.

Materials

Because public buildings last for generations, only durable, low-maintenance materials should be used for exterior finishes.

TRANSPORTATION FUNDAMENTALS

It is too often overlooked that pedestrian-friendly streets are an essential feature in successful urban transformations, and can be a major attractor for investors and the public. An important challenge for cities is to provide streets that are pedestrian-friendly.

Complete Streets

Approximately 40% of the land area in a typical downtown is occupied by paved roads and sidewalks. This land ownership ratio—40% public and 60% private—presents both an opportunity and a challenge. If the streets are pedestrian-friendly, the downtown will thrive; if the streets are pedestrian-hostile, the city is a negligent custodian of the public realm.

In response to climate change, cities and towns increasingly recognize the need to reduce reliance on the automobile, and to provide convenient means of public transportation.

The concept of a complete street includes all modes of transportation—including pedestrians, bicycles, automobiles, trucks, and all forms of public transit. In this mix, the pedestrian should always be the top priority.

Sometimes it can be difficult to find a firm that specializes in transportation engineering and does not adhere to the belief that the automobile should be the priority when designing streets. I have frequently had the experience of preparing concept designs for pedestrian-friendly streets, turning them over to an engineering firm to produce the final contract documents, and then finding that features intended to promote pedestrian use and comfort are removed.

Most city public works departments and state departments of transportation are staffed with people conditioned to believe that their primary responsibility is to accommodate the ever-increasing demand for automobile travel. To make matters worse, transportation consultants who work for public agencies are reluctant to do anything that will jeopardize their ability to secure the next lucrative contract for a road-related project. It is often considered a heresy for a transportation engineering firm to advocate for improving pedestrian or bicycle systems at the expense of the automobile. Citizens and officials would be well served by understanding these underlying dynamics that may be at play.

Complete Street Fundamentals

Urban Complete Street

Pedestrians

In healthy, vibrant cities the pedestrian should be the priority for street designers. If not, the pedestrian will get what's left over after the demands for accommodating automobiles and trucks have been satisfied. A street in which the pedestrian is comfortable is one designed for the most vulnerable—children, the elderly, and the handicapped.

Most communities want to make sidewalks and intersections pedestrian-friendly. A good beginning is to provide wide sidewalks, curbside parking that separates pedestrians from moving traffic, and curb extensions to reduce crossing distances at intersections. In addition, storefronts and lively building facades should front the sidewalk. Blank walls, drive-through banks, and parking lots all diminish the pedestrian experience.

Bicycles

Bicycles are one of the most cost-effective and environmentally friendly means of transportation. Research indicates that, at best, only roughly seven percent of the population will ride a bicycle alongside automobiles or on streets with painted bicycle lanes. The reason for this reluctance is that people fear serious injury from automobiles. Studies show that the only reliable way to bike safely is on protected bikeways, sometimes referred to as cycle tracks.

In many European communities extensive protected bicycle networks connect neighborhoods to major shopping and employment destinations. In these cities and towns, as many as 40–50% of all transportation trips are made by bicycle.

Automobiles and Trucks

The noise and commotion associated with heavy traffic discourages pedestrian activity. Mitigating the negative impacts of traffic by limiting automobile speeds, slowing traffic by converting one-way streets into two-way streets, and reducing the number of traffic lanes—a "road diet,"—goes a long way toward creating pedestrian-friendly streets.

Public Transit

Complete streets are designed to accommodate public transit. Transit stops should be integrated into the street design without compromising or restricting pedestrian circulation.

Location

Not every street can or should be a complete street. Some existing streets don't have sufficient right-of-way, and others don't connect neighborhoods to employment and shopping destinations. Budget constraints can also prevent the creation of a complete street.

For new development, an important first step in creating a complete street is to identify a network of streets that connect neighborhoods to trip generators (employment and shopping) and to include protected bikeways along those streets.

Character

A complete street will provide features that are typically not found on city streets. These include wider sidewalks, attractive landscaping, artwork, and human-scaled lighting. Other characteristics include special bicycle signals located at intersections to help eliminate bicycle and automobile conflicts and safer, shorter pedestrian crossings at intersections.

Public Transit

Ideally, public transit will be available within a five-minute walk from any location in a city.

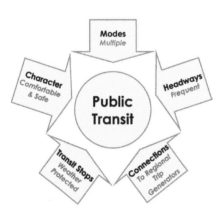

Public Transit Fundamentals

Public Transit

The secret to improving the use of public transit is to provide (1) dependable arrival and departure times, (2) a reasonable amount of travel time to reach a destination, and (3) connections to desirable work and shopping areas. Achieving these goals will be more likely if transit has an exclusive right-of-way that connects to major employment and shopping destinations.

Communities that wisely invest in light rail and modern streetcar systems sometimes overlook the importance of updating their plans and ordinances so that they incorporate sufficient development densities along the rail alignments. Without density, ridership does not materialize and the transit lines risk operating at a deficit.

Modes

Taxis, buses, Bus Rapid Transit (BRT), and Light Rail Transit (LRT) are the most common modes of public transit.

BRT, promoted as an alternative to constructing a LRT system, entails running buses in lanes reserved exclusively for bus use. BRT is cheaper to build than LRT and so is often attractive to city administrators. However, the downside of a proposed BRT system is that buses may be forced to intermingle with traffic if street size is not sufficiently wide, resulting in congestion and delays which will discourage ridership.

Streetcars, which share traffic lanes with automobiles, have special station platforms built exclusively for them. These platforms engage the tracks at fixed stops with multiple door openings, enabling rapid loading and unloading of passengers. The latest trend is to locate streetcars in exclusive, dedicated lanes.

Connections

To reduce dependency on the automobile, public transit must connect neighborhoods to employment and shopping destinations.

Arrival and Departure Interval

The maximum wait time between arrivals and departures for public transit is fifteen minutes. Waiting any longer tends to discourage ridership.

Transit Stops

Unfortunately, not all transit agencies do a good job of providing weather protection at transit stops. Waiting for transit with minimal protection from rain, wind, or cold is a disincentive.

Character

Traveling on public transit should feel comfortable and safe. Comfort is associated with good seating, a clean environment, and a controlled temperature. A safe environment is harder to define. Almost everyone has had the misfortune of riding with individuals who are intoxicated, on drugs, disorderly, or mentally ill. Such experiences cannot be completely avoided. An active transit security force that monitors passenger behavior can create a sense of security.

IMPLEMENTATION FUNDAMENTALS

Every Framework Plan requires an implementation strategy. At a minimum an implementation strategy should:

- stimulate downtown economic development
- revitalize downtown retail
- expand housing opportunities for all income groups
- position the downtown to be resilient to the impacts of climate change

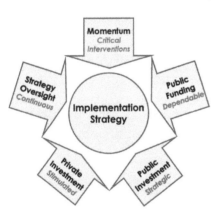

Implementation Strategy Fundamentals

Public Investment

Momentum

One of the primary functions of an implementation strategy is to create immediate momentum for implementing the Transformation Strategy. Unless the public sees significant progress within the first five years after a Transformation Strategy has been adopted, the plan will ultimately have little chance to succeed.

Urban designers like to prepare twenty-five-year plans. Such plans are less worrisome, because any proposed changes will only happen in the distant future, if at all. It is non-threatening but is also a non-plan. In twenty-five years' time, most everyone actively involved with the city—the politicians, the planning staff, and public activists—will very likely have moved on. Institutional memory will have faded, and advocacy for implementing the plan's recommendations will be nonexistent.

Some implementation strategies identify hundreds of items that need to be put into action, with no established priority for which items should be implemented first. Most public agencies, however, are not capable of handling more than a few tasks at a time—so such a strategy will not lead to success. It is far preferable to stipulate that no more than half a dozen high-priority projects be undertaken within the first five years. Identifying a limited number of projects for implementation allows the community to focus their attention and resources on the most critical interventions.

Public Funding

When I make public presentations around the country, I've come to expect that at some time fairly early on in the planning process, a florid-faced audience member, perhaps a little tipsy from the cocktail hour, will rise unsteadily to his feet, jab a finger in my direction, and ask, "So how are we gonna pay for all of this?"

Though the questioner is often hostile to any suggestion that may entail taxpayers' money, the question is always welcomed. With rare exceptions, the answer should be found in the Framework Plan itself, if it is bold enough. Any proposed public project should be of sufficient merit to stimulate substantial private investment; otherwise, it should be re-evaluated. But even cities with the most blighted downtowns in desperate need of transformation will often respond in horror at the suggestion that a strong public hand is required to reclaim the city. In my experience the revenues to fund public improvements always show up when substantial private investment opportunities are created.

The single most important part of any implementation strategy is the identification of funding sources for proposed public improvements. One key funding mechanism is Tax Increment Financing (TIF) and its variations. Tax Increment Financing works by taking advantage of anticipated future tax revenues based on the assumption that property values and, consequently, property tax receipts will reliably rise in and around substantive public improvements, provided the improvements are intelligently conceived and carried out. The anticipated growth in tax receipts can then be pledged against revenue bonds, thereby ensuring a project is properly capitalized. In 1961, voters in Oregon approved Tax Increment Financing, which turned out to be the single most valuable step toward Portland's later renaissance.

The rule of thumb is that one dollar of public money should stimulate at least five to seven dollars of private investment. The tax revenues from the private investment will then be sufficient to pay off the bond. The ratio of public to private investment varies in every tax jurisdiction, though the above rule of thumb applies almost everywhere.

Many city officials, elected or otherwise, do not fully appreciate how important the investment of public dollars is for bringing private money into the transformation effort. A public investment should be thought of as a pebble thrown into a calm pond, causing ever-extending ripples of private investment.

Another common obstacle to successful transformation is the burden of previous financial commitments. Public monies may be tied up with a pet project of the mayor, city staff, or a well-connected developer. These types of project will differ from community to community, but they all share the potential for sucking up precious public resources without stimulating ongoing private investment. Consequently, they delay or even kill projects that would make a substantive difference in a community.

Whatever the source of funds for public improvements, it is crucial that their availability be dependable over an extended period of time. An ongoing struggle to find money for strategic public improvements can stall or stop implementation momentum altogether.

Of course, even the most carefully conceived financing program cannot in itself transform a city on its own. It must be wedded to an equally well-considered physical design produced during the preparation of a Framework Plan.

Public Investment

Every city has a unique set of needs, and strategic public investments will vary accordingly. In my experience, public investments can be identified only through a rigorous planning process in which a number of alternatives are evaluated and prioritized and in which the public is involved in decision making. There are few exceptions to this funda-mental principle.

The first consideration should always be the choice of a public project in which to invest. Typically, the project should provide ameni-ties that are lacking and offer the potential to improve the quality of life in the city. It may be an improvement to the pedestrian environ-ment that stimulates retail development or it may be a park or open space that creates a pleasant and welcoming investment environment. A central plaza that provides a place for public assembly and events is another possibility, as is a public parking structure that accommodates downtown shoppers and workers.

I am often asked where museums and performing arts centers fit in the hierarchy of public expenditures. Cultural non-profit institutions do not generate tax revenues or stimulate private investment, at least not initially, and they should not be a top priority unless a city has the capacity to absorb negative cash flow. Expenditures for most cul-tural facilities should wait until a later phase of transformation, when fundamental downtown public investments have been made, and pri-vate investment is on the upswing. Timing is everything for successful urban transformation.

Private Investment

An effective implementation strategy will stimulate substantial private investment, such as office buildings, hotels, retail facilities, and high-density housing.

Many elected officials cling to the unfounded belief that the market will somehow allocate resources efficiently, with favorable results for all. Consequently, it is often taken as an article of faith that, for the greater good, developers should be given the final word about what is to be built, and how, and where. This philosophy, regrettably, has produced many blighted downtowns and failed or abandoned transfor-mation plans all over the country.

Strategy Oversight

Adoption of an implementation strategy is simply the first step in an effort to transform a city. The next step is to appoint or assign responsibility for overseeing the implementation activities to a public oversight committee for a period of five years. Members of the oversight committee should include government leaders, respected business leaders, and a variety of interest groups.

This is a critical final step because planning staffs cannot be relied on to implement a plan. They do not have political clout, they may not be able to withstand the political pressures that accompany implementation, and they often move on to other staff positions or jobs.

THE BUSINESS CASE

The business case is a valuable decision-making tool that describes the financial implications of different development scenarios.

A business case includes:

- build-out plans
- build-out illustrations
- development summaries
- a financial analysis

Build-out Plan

A build-out plan is prepared by assuming that all undeveloped and low-valued parcels of land in a study area will be developed or redeveloped over time.

The process is not complicated. Plans are prepared with consideration given to:

- fundamental urban design principles
- market demand
- land use
- realistic building footprints
- neighborhood context

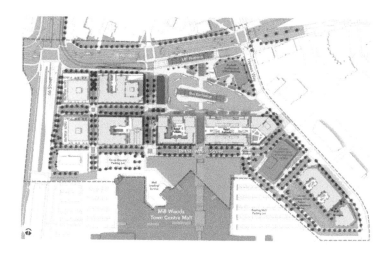

Build-out Plan

Build-out Illustration

Three-dimensional drawings that illustrate the build-out plan are prepared. They identify building:

- placement
- occupancy
- character
- height

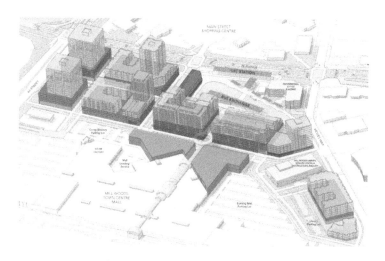

Build-out Illustration

Development Summary

Tables are also prepared. They quantify:

- the areas for buildings and parking
- the right-of-way improvements
- the public investment
- the value of private investment

Financial Analysis

The financial analysis includes:

- anticipated annual tax revenues that will result from private investment
- the expected payback period for the public

Business Case Scenarios

The Edmonton Stadium Station Redevelopment Project in Canada illustrates how a business case functions in the process of transformation.

Stadium Station, which opened in 1978, is one of five original stations built as part of Edmonton's Light Rail Transit system. It is located in close proximity to Commonwealth Stadium. Thirty years after the LRT system became operational, the station was still surrounded by vacant properties. In 2013, Edmonton decision-makers asked my firm to prepare a redevelopment strategy that would stimulate private investment around the station. They wanted to see a range of scenarios that would illustrate the financial implications of various development densities and circulation alternatives. The business case provided the information they needed to make an informed decision.

The Stadium Station business case evaluation included three scenarios:

Scenario One: The induced market scenario entailed the greatest public investment in order to stimulate the highest private investment. A strategic public improvement—in this case, a retail Main Street—was the intervention that was identified.

Scenario Two: The enhanced market scenario entailed some public investment—a public square and street improvements—to enhance existing properties and make them more attractive to the development community.

Scenario Three: The market trend scenario assumed no public investment would be provided, and developers would assume responsibility
for constructing any necessary infrastructure. The absence of public
amenities would make properties less attractive to the development
community.

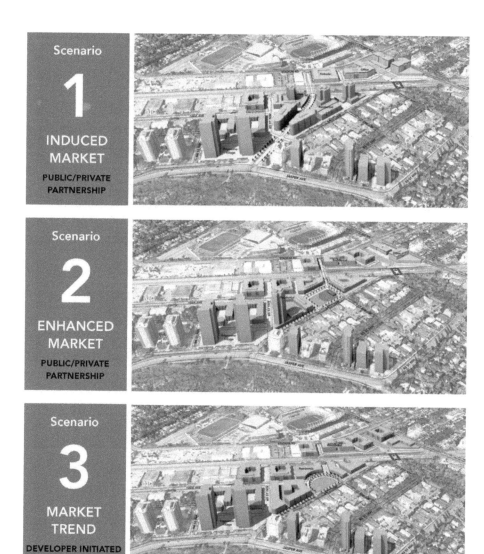

Business Case Scenarios

Scenario Comparison

Scenario One was designed to attract the largest amount of private investment, and included:

- a Main Street that would provide much-needed retail and commercial amenities in the underserved area
- a new rail crossing that would connect new development to adjacent neighborhoods and the major regional fitness center, sports facilities, and stadium located there

The public investment was estimated to be approximately $10 million.

Scenario Two would not include a retail Main Street, but would provide a new rail crossing and a public square. The public investment associated with this scenario was estimated to be approximately $7.7 million.

Scenario Three would not include a Main Street, rail crossing, or a public square. It was based on no public investment whatsoever. Letting the market decide would result in the least amount of private investment.

1 INDUCED MARKET	PRIVATE INVESTMENT (BUILD-OUT)	$	374,309,843
	ANNUAL TAX REVENUE @ BUILD-OUT	$	2,871,239
	PUBLIC INVESTMENT	$	10,022,040
	PAYBACK PERIOD*		12 YEARS
2 ENHANCED MARKET	PRIVATE INVESTMENT (BUILD-OUT)	$	298,398,985
	ANNUAL TAX REVENUE @ BUILD-OUT	$	1,937,743
	PUBLIC INVESTMENT	$	7,682,011
	PAYBACK PERIOD*	$	10 YEARS
3 MARKET TREND	PRIVATE INVESTMENT (BUILD-OUT)	$	144,530,841
	ANNUAL TAX REVENUE @ BUILD-OUT	$	959,984
	PUBLIC INVESTMENT	$	0
	PAYBACK PERIOD*		0

Business Case Summary

Business Case Summary

City decision-makers and developers reviewed the business case summary and favored the increased development potential in Scenarios One and Two. Developers preferred Scenario Two because they felt that the retail Main Street in Scenario One might be difficult to implement. A decision was made to implement Scenario Two.

Everyone agreed that Scenario Three (leaving development to the whims of the market) would have occurred if the business case had not been prepared. The business case illustrated that public investment in Scenario Two would result in more than double the private investment resulting from Scenario Three.

Mixed-Use

"Mixed-use" is a term planners use to refer to land uses that contain a variety of activity, such as retail, commercial, institutional, and housing. Mixed-use development can occur horizontally or vertically. A horizontal mix means that a housing project could be built adjacent to an office building. A vertical mix means that housing, employment, or retail uses can be stacked on top of one another in a single building.

The term "mixed-use" is often misused to avoid the hard work of determining exactly which land uses would work best in a city and precisely where they should be located. The term can end up being simply another way of saying "let the market decide."

A wrong mix can devalue the project's contribution to the urban environment and the developer's investment. For example, most people would prefer to live in a residential neighborhood, not in an employment district. Most employers also generally prefer to locate their place of business in an employment district, not in a residential neighborhood. When these two uses are mixed together, the results may not always be successful. In general, a random horizontal mix of land uses can lead to degradation of the urban environment. A vertical mix can also present problems. Most people would prefer not to live in an office building and most employers would prefer not to locate their offices in a building that contains housing.

In the absence of a plan that designates exactly where retail would thrive, retail tends to be randomly scattered throughout an area, which is never as healthy as having a concentration of retail.

It goes without saying that a city is inevitably a mix of land uses. The healthiest, most vibrant urban environments have concentrations of housing in the form of neighborhoods and concentrations of employment in other areas. The seams between housing neighborhoods and employment centers are transition areas that require special attention. The seam may be a good place to locate Main Street retail and shops or to insert park blocks to create separation between employment and residential areas. The seam might also be an area where mixed-use work-live buildings make sense. Designating large expanses of a city as suitable for mixed-uses, on the other hand, may lead to degradation, reduce the attractiveness of private investment, and diminish the quality of life.

GAME CHANGERS

Game changers are public investments that stimulate private development momentum. It is vital that a Framework Plan contain game changers—for without them, it will not succeed.

Game Changer Fundamentals

Game Changers: 1972 Portland Downtown Plan

Typical game changers are strategically located and visually prominent projects, such as plazas and parks. Improvements to the transportation system that create pedestrian-friendly streets or open up land for redevelopment are also game changers. Projects that are not part of the built environment—such as market studies, parking studies, branding exercises, or promotional campaigns—do not qualify as game changers because they are invisible to investors and the public.

Because every city and town is different, an appropriate, effective game changer can be identified only through a systematic design exercise. Every completed Framework Plan should include the identification of game changers and a schedule for their implementation.

Momentum

A game changer has the potential to stimulate substantial private investment within five years after its completion. In order to create a game changer, cities may sometimes link the expenditure of public funds with private investor agreements that commit private investors to follow up with specific construction projects once the game changer project is under way or completed.

Location

For a game changer to be successful, location is critical. For example, a public plaza sited on the edge of the downtown in an undesirable neighborhood will do little to stimulate private investment, even though the plaza may be a welcome addition to a city. If it is located in the center of the city, however, it can be expected to attract significant private investment in the immediate vicinity.

Public Perception

When a game changer is built, it changes the public's perception of the city. In the past, people may have had little inclination or need to visit a downtown, but after construction of the game changer, the public will be attracted. The public's perception will be that the city is changing for the better.

Private Investment

Game changers are interventions that attract private investment. Investors and developers understand that a game changer will create investment opportunities and increase property values.

Public Investment

Before public funds are spent on a game changer, the public investment return should be estimated. A rule of thumb is that every public dollar spent on a game changer should stimulate at least five to seven dollars in private investment. Typically that ratio will generate enough tax revenue to pay off the public investment in a reasonable amount of time.

Portland Game Changers

In 1970, downtown Portland was a grimy, amorphous grid, with almost no commercial allure. It was not at all certain that it could be redeemed under any circumstances. Portland was in desperate need of an urban intervention to reverse its downtown economic decline. A small group of civic activists realized that it was time to stop talking and to start putting together a plan that summarized the community's aspirations. The result was the 1972 Downtown Plan. Of the twenty-three projects proposed in the plan, three became game changers, altering the investor and public perception of the downtown—from an undesirable backwater to an exciting and vibrant place to be.

The three game changers were the Transit Mall, Waterfront Park, and Pioneer Courthouse Square. Ironically, they were presented in the last few pages of the plan, almost as an afterthought. If they had not been proposed and implemented, Portland would not be the highly livable, attractive city that it is today. In many ways Portland has been lucky.

The Transit Mall and Waterfront Park, both completed in 1978, transformed downtown Portland from a place to avoid to a place where everyone wanted to be. What was missing was a central public space that could function as a stage for celebrations and public events. That need was satisfied in 1984 with completion of Pioneer Courthouse Square.

Portland Game Changer One: Transit Mall

While I was working for Skidmore, Owings & Merrill (SOM), we were hired to design the Transit Mall for downtown Portland. The mall was going to be located on eleven blocks on two parallel streets—twenty-two blocks in all. Our design entailed widening the sidewalks, paving them with brick, and adding landscaping, benches, public art, and attractive bus shelters.

Transit Mall Street: Before   Transit Mall: After

I remember some of my SOM colleagues saying to me, "The transit mall is going to be awful, because the buses are going to be very noisy." But I wasn't concerned about bus noise. All I really cared about was creating a downtown spine with widened brick sidewalks, landscaping, benches, banner poles, and public art that would attract the public.

As I had hoped, the moment plans for the proposed transit mall went public, smart private developers said, "Aha! Now we know where the action's going to be in downtown. Now we know where to build new projects." These developers understood that properties located along the transit mall would provide excellent investment potential, and they wisely cashed in on it. When the transit mall opened in 1978, several large building projects bordering the mall had already been completed or were under construction.

Portland Game Changer Two: Tom McCall Waterfront Park

The Willamette River, which bisects Portland, had long been isolated from the city's downtown by a seawall, and by a four-lane 1940s freeway known as Harbor Drive that ran alongside it. A traffic study had suggested that the freeway be expanded from four to six lanes to accommodate future growth. In 1968 Governor Tom McCall halted the expansion, called for removal of the freeway, and proposed building a waterfront park where the freeway had been. His recommendation was supported and promoted by Riverfront for People, a group of public activists who fought for public access to the river; and the Portland City Club, a prominent citizen-based research organization.

Tom McCall Waterfront Park Site: Before   Tom McCall Waterfront Park: After

In 1974, Harbor Drive was closed. It was the first major highway in America to be intentionally removed and not replaced. In 1978 a thirty-seven-acre riverfront park named after the farsighted governor was opened to rave reviews, and downtown Portland, now reconnected to the Willamette River, has never been the same. Tom McCall Waterfront Park has become the staging area for many city and regional events throughout the year, and generates a substantial stimulus to the local economy from expenditures by visitors and shoppers.

Portland Game Changer Three: Pioneer Courthouse Square

Portlanders had come to realize that their city, like all great cities, needed a well-defined, attractive focal point in the heart of its downtown—an open space that would be available for public events and assembly. San Francisco had its Union Square; *Piazza San Marco* is the familiar, well-loved center of Venice, Italy; and in Paris, there is the *Place de la Concorde*. Portland deserved a grand central plaza, too.

Pioneer Courthouse Square Site: Before   Pioneer Courthouse Square: After

A site was selected for Portland's signature plaza opposite the city's handsome nineteenth-century Italianate Pioneer Courthouse. At the time, a two-story parking garage owned by Meier & Frank, a Portland-based department store chain, occupied the block. In the late 1960s, Meier & Frank had wanted to erect an even bigger eleven-story garage on the site—a prospective disaster for the downtown that was barely averted. By transforming the space into what would become Pioneer Courthouse Square, the city settled the future of the site for good.

Not everyone was enthusiastic about the idea of creating a plaza. Many Portlanders thought it didn't make sense to establish an open space on a site where a parking structure already existed. They proposed finding a vacant lot somewhere else in the city to build the plaza—a cheaper approach, but ill-conceived. The whole point of a plaza is for it to be in the center of the city. Eventually, Meier & Frank was persuaded to relinquish the property in exchange for another site a few blocks away, where a parking structure would be built at the city's expense.

Then another concern surfaced. The mayor and his friends in the business community felt that the new square might attract undesirables to the downtown. They wanted half of the block devoted to an active use in order to mitigate any possible problems. Several ideas were put forth, including a conservatory. A nationwide design competition was held to select the architect for the square. Of the five entries, only one was from Portland, from local architect Will Martin. His scheme entailed leaving the entire block as open space. When the judges reviewed the submissions, it quickly became apparent that only one would work—Martin's. His design won the competition.

Unhappy with the outcome, the mayor refused to fund construction of Martin's design. This prompted a public outcry and the formation of a citizen-initiated campaign to raise money for the project. Several fund-raising innovations—including selling individual paving bricks that bore the donor's name, an idea that has since caught on all across the country—were successful, and Martin's popular design was built.

Pioneer Courthouse Square opened to the public on April 6, 1984, to widespread popular and critical acclaim. Fondly referred to as "Portland's living room," today the square hosts over 300 events annually and attracts nearly 10 million visitors each year.

Portland Game Changer Four: Lovejoy Ramp Removal

The 1988 Portland City Center Plan expanded the designated downtown area northward into what was then known as the "northwest industrial triangle." At the time the 253-acre area contained an abandoned railroad yard, warehouses, and light industrial enterprises. The Lovejoy Ramp, an elevated 1920s automobile viaduct, bisected the district.

In 1999, the viaduct was demolished and replaced with an on-grade roadway. Opening up the land for redevelopment led in turn to the creation of what is now known as the Pearl District. Today the Pearl has become a thriving, high-density, mixed-use neighborhood with a population of over 7,000 and employment for over 12,000.

Pearl District: Before   Pearl District: After

Portland Game Changer Five: Aerial Tram

The 1988 Central City Plan also expanded the designated downtown area southward, onto a 140-acre parcel of brownfield—land previously used for industrial purposes. South Waterfront, as the district is now known, is one of the largest urban redevelopment projects in the United States. From the beginning, the area had been envisioned as an urban mixed-use neighborhood with condominiums, apartments, and medical research facilities.

South Waterfront: Aerial Tram Location   Aerial Tram

Oregon Health & Science University (OHSU), which is situated above the South Waterfront district, on top of Marquam Hill to the west, had been looking for expansion space. The suburbs were an option, as was the South Waterfront area. The problem with the South Waterfront was its circuitous two-mile driving distance from the OHSU hilltop campus. As the bird flies, though, the two sites were

96

relatively close. The solution: build an aerial tramway to link the top of the hill with the waterfront. Construction of an aerial tramway was the catalyst that allowed that vision to become a reality.

The tram, completed in 2006 at a cost of $57 million, travels a distance of 3,300 feet, with a gain in elevation of 500 feet. While most passengers tend to be affiliated with OHSU, the tram is open to the public, and is popular for its easy access to the hilltop campus. Tourists enjoy splendid views of the city and Mt. Hood in the distance.

In 2004, mixed-use developments broke ground in the South Waterfront area. By 2014, seven residential towers, each between twenty-one and thirty floors high, and two OHSU medical buildings had been completed. Additional OHSU buildings, representing an investment of over $1 billion, are soon to follow.

The aerial tram enabled the landlocked OHSU campus on Marquam Hill to expand into the South Waterfront district over a half mile away—a move that created the potential for thousands of new jobs for healthcare workers and researchers. The development community correctly understood that the expanded medical facilities would translate into a substantial demand for more housing, and for commercial and retail space in close proximity to the buildings. Since the tram's completion, the South Waterfront has experienced explosive growth.

Game Changers in Other Cities

For every community, the type of game changer with the greatest potential for providing a major stimulus will be different. Whatever it is, the game changer should always be a part of larger, comprehensive redevelopment strategy, never a stand-alone project.

Marion Mall Street Renovation: Oak Park, Illinois

In Oak Park, Illinois, the game changer was the renovation of the street in Marion Mall, a pedestrian-only street. It had been trendy in the 1970s to create pedestrian-only shopping streets that were closed to automobile traffic. However, like many other communities that had tried this experiment, Oak Park did not have sufficient population density to support the street closure, and retail sales declined. Soon vacant storefronts were lining the street.

Marion Mall businesses were not the only businesses that had been impacted by the street closure. All of Oak Park's downtown retail suffered from the restricted automobile access the closure had created. Without convenient access, downtown shopping quickly declined.

Marion Mall: Before

Marion Street: After

When I proposed opening up Marion Mall as the first step in transforming downtown, Marion Mall businesses protested. A hair-dresser, for example, enjoyed having depressed rental rates. Because of the nature of his business, he didn't have to rely on either pedestrian traffic or drive-by automobile traffic. At one point in a public meeting he declared to the audience, "If Marion Mall is re-opened, leases will go up, and I'll be out of business." That was the sentiment of many of the remaining businesses on the street.

Obviously, no one wanted to create a situation in which long-time businesses would feel the pressure to relocate. But at the same time it was important to everyone concerned to improve the downtown's economy. In the end, the decision was made to re-open Marion Street, which underwent a major redesign. The reconstruction had a strong pedestrian bias and included wider sidewalks, on-street parking, land-scaping, and special lighting.

Ultimately, the street re-opening was a success for Marion Street and for the entire downtown. Improved automobile circulation attracted shoppers, and stimulated retail sales for everyone.

Street Transformation: Lake Oswego, Oregon

In Lake Oswego the game changer was a demonstration project intended to transform an automobile-dominated street into a pedes-trian-friendly one.

| A Street: Before | A Street: After |

Lake Oswego was typical of many suburban communities. Its downtown retail was scattered and lacked focus. I was convinced that an effective way to revitalize retail was to turn its A Avenue—a pedestrian-hostile, five-lane roadway through the middle of town—into a pedestrian-friendly street.

To test the idea, a one-block, two-intersection demonstration project was designed and constructed in front of City Hall. Curb extensions, landscaped medians, widened sidewalks, special street furniture, and lighting created an environment desirable to investors and shoppers. The four lanes of traffic and on-street parking would remain.

The project opened to rave reviews, and soon an additional three blocks were completed, as well as the construction of more retail projects on A Avenue and the intersecting streets. Lake Oswego now has a distinctive downtown that regularly draws people to its many shops and restaurants.

Park Blocks: Medford, Oregon

The game changer in Medford, Oregon, was the design of Middleford Commons, a series of new park blocks that were built in a partially abandoned downtown warehouse district. The City of Medford had come to the realization that unless it had a plan to redevelop the warehouse area, development would be piecemeal and not supportive of downtown transformation, the city's ultimate aim.

My firm suggested organizing new development around a set of three park blocks connected to Main Street. We specified exactly the types of stores, housing, and other structures to be built, and provided schematic drawings of each type to illustrate precisely what was needed. We had estimated the total cost for building the park blocks at around $10 million, and forecast that, in return, approximately $150 million in new private investment would be generated. Unfortunately, $10 million was more than Medford could afford.

Middleford Commons Site: Before

Middleford Commons Site: After

As it turned out, Lithia Motors, a major national car dealership with a number of retail outlets across the city, owned several of the blocks slated to become park blocks, and they had announced their intention to build an auto mall and company headquarters on the outskirts of town. Then a remarkable thing happened. When Lithia management saw the plan for the park blocks, they liked the scheme so much that they changed their mind and decided to locate their new headquarters building alongside the proposed park blocks. Also, they believed that the park blocks would help them solve another of their problems. According to their national recruiting efforts, the majority of desirable job candidates preferred to live in a downtown, not in the suburbs. The park blocks plan would be perfect for them.

Because the cost of building the park blocks was beyond the City of Medford's budget, Lithia offered to pay for construction, with the agreement that the city would pay them back with the tax increments generated by the construction of other new buildings that were sure to come. The parks blocks have been built along with the first phase of Lithia's headquarters complex, and Medford has benefited significantly—transforming a backwater in the city to a desirable place to live and work.

SILVER BULLETS

I refer to public actions with long-term negative political and/or financial impacts as "silver bullets." I call them silver bullets because they are a product of magical thinking—we think they are going to be the cure for an ailing city, but in fact they often end up making things worse. For cities to stay healthy, they need to dodge the silver bullets that show up from time to time.

Silver Bullets: Magical Thinking

Silver bullet projects are often sold to the public as game changers. Sometimes they are the pet project of the governor, the mayor, a member of the city staff, or a well-respected developer. Silver bullets differ from community to community, but they all share the same potential for using precious public financial resources without stimulating ongoing private investment. Consequently, they delay, or even terminate, other projects that could make a real difference to a community. Major damage to a city can be avoided if silver bullets are identified and stopped before a single shovelful of dirt is turned over.

Silver bullets will be inevitable if a city does not have a Transformation Strategy in place that creates a framework for effective decision-making. In the absence of such a framework, decisions regarding land use and transportation issues will be little more than guesswork.

Portland's Silver Bullets

Mount Hood Freeway

An excellent example of a dodged silver bullet is the Mt. Hood Freeway project that was proposed for Portland in the 1970s. The original plan, prepared by the Oregon Department of Transportation (ODOT) in 1955, called for 9.2 miles of freeway to cut through Portland's eastside neighborhoods. In 1969 construction was ready to begin at a cost of $500 million, funded by a mix of 90% federal funds and 10% state and local revenues. The last hurdle before work could begin was the preparation of an environmental impact statement (EIS) in order to comply with the 1969 National Environmental Protection Act.

In 1971 ODOT hired the Portland office of Skidmore, Owings & Merrill (SOM) to prepare the EIS. Personnel from SOM's Baltimore office who had relevant experience with freeway studies were transferred to Portland to work on the project. Knowing almost nothing about freeways but with a degree in civil engineering, I was recruited to join the team.

The Mt. Hood Freeway project was typical of the dynamics often associated with large transportation studies. Transportation engineering firms with a fundamental conflict of interest are often retained as consultants, and this project was no exception. This is how it works: state transportation agencies serve as the client for freeway construction, and they expect that transportation consultants preparing EIS materials will understand that the task at hand is to deliver good news to promote the project. Bad news could halt a project. Transportation consultants are, of course, keenly aware that state agencies may not consider them for future projects if their EIS findings are unfavorable.

ODOT had assigned "minders" to the Mt. Hood EIS study. The job of the minder was to be on the lookout for anything that might be viewed as negative in the EIS. If they found something questionable, they were to edit the text and sanitize the findings.

There were other problems. The transportation sub-consultants who had been hired to assist the SOM team were biased in favor of the

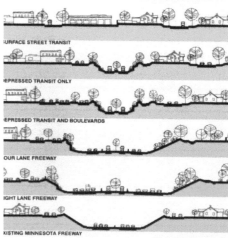

Proposed Mount Hood Freeway   Mount Hood Freeway Options

freeway, and they tried to make the numbers in support of construction look particularly good. For example, the subconsultants projected travel times with computer models—but these projections were not accurate. To address the resulting inconsistencies, I would often have to sit down with them and negotiate more accurate figures.

As one of the EIS Project Managers, I had to figure out how to splice the planned new roadway into Portland's existing freeway system. The unspoken truth was that the problem could never be solved, because the existing freeway loop simply did not have the capacity to accommodate the anticipated traffic demands.

The Mt. Hood Freeway EIS was published in 1973, with the title, *I-80 N Environmental Study, Freeway Design Alternatives, Volume 1.* A separate report, entitled *A Range of Options, Volume 2,* outlined alternative options to building the freeway—such as transit-based solutions and other roadway configurations that included transit.

The EIS report made it very clear that the trade-off for a modest reduction in time travel was a massive disruption to the eastside neighborhoods—the displacement of 1,700 homes and 5,000 people. Oregon decision-makers carefully studied the EIS findings and wisely pulled the plug on the project. And just as importantly, they succeeded in convincing the federal government to transfer approximately $180 million of the funds that had been allocated to the Mt. Hood Freeway towards construction of a Light Rail Transit (LRT) system for Portland.

The decision to not build the freeway turned what would have been a silver bullet into a game changer. Having the federal monies to construct a LRT system marked the beginning of Portland's shift from total reliance on the automobile to something far saner and more environmentally sound—a convenient, state-of-the-art public transit system for bringing people into the city center. If the freeway had been built, the already congested freeway system would have become virtually non-functional, Portland's downtown would have been choked with traffic, and the benefits of light rail would have been compromised and delayed for years. It took courage for Oregon decision-makers to turn down the freeway when funding was already in the bank, but the payoff for downtown Portland has been enormous—cleaner air and more than 40% of all downtown employees arriving by transit.

Columbia River Crossing

Oregon and Washington share the banks of the Columbia River, which serves as a border between the two states. Portland is on one side of the river and Vancouver on the other. Traffic between the neighboring cities can become quite congested. A six-lane truss bridge connects the two metropolises. To ease congestion, the Oregon and Washington Departments of Transportation proposed constructing a replacement bridge, which became known as the Columbia River Crossing (CRC).

In addition to improving the flow of traffic, the proposed new bridge would be built to current seismic standards, an important consideration in the earthquake-prone region. Planning and design of the CRC commenced in 2005, and by 2013, $200 million had been spent. But in June of that year, the project was terminated. What went wrong?

The CRC had been undertaken as a much-needed transportation improvement, but over time it became a silver bullet project that needed to be stopped. First, during the planning and design process a fundamental step had been ignored—the inclusion of alternative options for public evaluation. Only one solution to the problem had been proposed—the one embraced by the people working on the project. Other points of view were missing.

Also, with an estimated final cost of $3.4 billion, the proposed bridge was simply not affordable, and further evaluation revealed that the scheme did not meet the project's primary objective, which was to relieve congestion. Most troubling of all, because of the proposed bridge's substandard height, it would obstruct some boats from traveling along the river.

Proposed Bridge (CRC)

The public quickly understood that the CRC was seriously flawed, and objected to its construction. Other solutions that worked better and saved billions of dollars were developed and promoted by citizen activists. For example, the Common Sense Alternative (CSA), which I helped develop, cost less than one third of the CRC's total $3.4 billion budget. Nonetheless, thanks to a massive lobbying campaign funded by various labor and business interests, the CRC was approved by the Oregon legislature. Fortunately, Washington's legislature turned it down.

By dodging this silver bullet, both Oregon and Washington avoided the serious depletion of their already scarce highway funds, as well as a number of destructive impacts from the CRC—including increased traffic congestion on other routes as motorists tried to avoid the expensive toll bridge, the obstruction of river traffic from the low-hung bridge, and increased air pollution in neighboring North Portland communities.

Silver Bullets in Other Cities

Competing Retail Center: Lincoln, Nebraska

Every city has its share of silver bullet projects. In Lincoln, Nebraska, a capitol city with approximately a quarter of a million people situated among rolling hills in the southeastern corner of the state, I encountered the ambitious Antelope Valley Plan. The project was intended to transform a large area on the eastern edge of downtown Lincoln into a type of retail development known as a "lifestyle center."

Like shopping malls, which are indoor versions of old Main Street shops, lifestyle centers are like movie sets—outdoor malls that masquerade as uniquely themed historical Main Streets or as European-like town squares, with shopping, dining, and entertainment.

The problem with lifestyle centers is that, like suburban malls, they compete for retailers and suck the life out of downtown main streets. They also increase dependency on the automobile because they are accessible only by car. Professional planners, nevertheless, find them hard to resist, as was the case in Lincoln.

One of the cardinal rules of transformation is to save the heart first. In other words, it is more important to focus transformation efforts first in the core of a city. The central downtown is where the history of a city lies and where its heart is. So when my firm was retained to produce a downtown Transformation Strategy for Lincoln, I told city officials the Antelope Valley project would be like a knife to the heart of downtown. It might have been comparatively easy to build a new retail center on the edge of downtown, but the Antelope Valley lifestyle center would have absorbed all retail business from downtown for many years to come. Fortunately, city officials understood the conflict and Lincoln's silver bullet was eventually dropped.

Condominium Project: Oak Park, Illinois

When we began preparing a downtown Framework Plan for Oak Park, a suburb of Chicago and birthplace of writer Ernest Hemingway, we found that the city had committed to a silver bullet. The project was a private mixed-use condominium development that required a large expenditure of public funds in order to proceed. The public was upset, and rightly so, with the proposed expenditure of public money on a private project.

Since the condominiums would leverage very little additional private investment, my candid advice was to ditch the project. This advice, unfortunately, was too late in coming. In time, to express their displeasure, the public voted out the village board members who had approved the condominiums.

Competing Plan: Casper, Wyoming

In Casper, Wyoming, the silver bullet was a major planning effort for an area adjacent to the downtown known as the Old Yellowstone District. The plan had just been completed when my firm was hired to prepare a Downtown Transformation Strategy. It soon became clear that the Old Yellowstone District plan would be in conflict with our efforts to revive the downtown core. If implemented, some of the proposed land uses for the Old Yellowstone District would end up degrading the potential for the downtown's future development.

This problem is typical of what happens in many cities. Plans are developed for areas adjacent to the downtown without first resolving what needs to happen in the core. Piecemeal planning and out-of-sequence planning efforts produce silver bullets.

CHAPTER FIVE

Implementation Rules

Without Implementation Rules, a Framework Plan will be ineffective.

Astoria is a historic Oregon fishing community at the mouth of the Columbia River. The town is filled with Victorian homes and the river's edge is lined with remnants of the canneries that once processed the bountiful salmon harvests.

My firm had been retained to prepare a master plan for the reuse of a large, vacant industrial site in the downtown. During the planning process, the public expressed its concern about the changing character of their downtown. The statement that we heard again and again was, "Our city is starting to look like every other city. We need to do something to protect our unique character."

Our first step was to identify the design vocabulary that made Astoria unique. A unifying architectural feature was the dark grey roofs found on both homes and canneries. It was obvious that contemporary buildings with their multi-colored metal roofs—reds, blues, greens, and yellows—were seriously eroding the town's character. There were no design guidelines in place in Astoria, and it was clear they were needed.

We made our final presentation for master plan approval to the City Council. I hadn't expected much of a turnout because the council chamber was small and a winter storm was dumping rain on Astoria. I was surprised to see people arriving early to get a seat. By the time the meeting started, it was standing room only.

I concluded my presentation with the comment, "Your next step should be to prepare design guidelines and initiate a design review process." The mayor, who was a local businessman, blurted out, "Over my dead body." The shocked audience sat in silence and then someone yelled out, "Everyone in favor of design guidelines and design review, raise your hands." Every hand in the audience shot up. Some raised two hands.

The mayor's reaction was not unusual. Businessmen and developers often consider design review a time-consuming and costly inconvenience. Architects often see it as an unwelcome interference into their world of design expertise. If the public could be assured that developers and architects would be responsive to the larger community context, then design review would not be necessary. The reality is that developers and architects have their own goals and cannot be relied upon to determine what is most appropriate for a city.

Astoria now has design guidelines and a design review process in place. New buildings are compatible with historic structures, and the special ambiance of Astoria is being preserved.

Implementation Rules
Policies, Regulations, and Design Guidelines

Framework Plan
Retail, Employment, Housing, Civic Uses,
Open Space, Complete Streets,
Implementation

Public Support

Transformation Strategy Basic Elements

THE NEED FOR RULES

Implementation rules provide the guidelines and standards needed to ensure that the intent of the Framework Plan is achieved. They tend to be the missing component in many planning efforts, yet they are an essential requirement if a Transformation Strategy is to be successful. Implementation rules include design guidelines, design standards, and public area standards.

- Design guidelines protect investment and ensure quality.
- Design standards identify essential requirements for private development.
- Public area standards specify streetscape and open space standards and details.

Like a house, the three basic elements of a Transformation Strategy provide a foundation, an enclosure, and a roof. The implementation rules are the roof—a necessary component that protects the integrity of the completed Framework Plan once it has been adopted.

In the absence of a Framework Plan, some communities will rely on rules and codes alone. Although this is another way to address transformation issues, the rules tend to be abstract, arbitrary, and ineffective, because a detailed Framework Plan does not inform them.

Implementation rules have a number of benefits. They put into place measures that enhance a downtown's appearance and livability. More importantly, they create economic vitality by attracting investors looking for opportunities in which the rules are clearly defined and risk is minimized.

Implementation rules, at their best, prevent undesirable change, and encourage desirable change. Undesirable change can include buildings that are incompatible in design, scale, or character with downtown neighborhoods or perhaps roadway improvements that create a hostile pedestrian environment.

Three Types of Cities

Cities can be categorized into three types:

Dynamic Cities

The public likes to visit dynamic cities. Buildings and streets are designed to enhance the pedestrian experience. Building facades and scale are compatible with adjacent buildings and the surrounding neighborhood. Parking structures are attractive, with cars hidden from view. Blank walls at the street level are avoided or absent altogether. A large population lives in the central core and has convenient access to employment opportunities, a vibrant retail environment, restaurants, and entertainment. There are plentiful quality-of-life features, such as parks, open spaces, cultural facilities, and recreational opportunities. A dynamic city feels safe at all hours of the day and night and is a great place to live, do business, and visit.

Dynamic cities do not happen by chance. They are a result of an effective Framework Plan and implementation rules.

Ordinary Cities

Cities that have few or no distinguishing features or places of beauty are not attractive to visitors. They may be old cities or newer suburban cities. They are automobile-dominated and pedestrian-hostile.

An old city may once have been considered dynamic, but through the years it may have been degraded. One-of-a-kind historic buildings may have been demolished to make way for parking lots and undistinguished newer buildings. Roadways were widened to accommodate automobiles, and the pedestrian environment was compromised. Employment opportunities declined as employers left the core area. And sooner or later, downtown retail shops moved out to the mall.

Ordinary cities can become dynamic cities with an effective Framework Plan and implementation rules.

Terminal Cities

The public and investors may choose to not visit or do business in a terminal city. Development in its central core creates a hostile pedestrian environment. New office buildings with blank walls, parking structures with inactive ground floors, and mini-plazas line the streets. Downtown shopping opportunities are limited, and downtown housing is scarce. Large roadways and freeways dominate the use of land. Public transit is limited. After workers leave, the downtown is empty.

Cities risk becoming terminal when the let-the-market-decide philosophy is allowed to shape the urban environment. Unlike ordinary cities, terminal cities are difficult to repair. The substantial investment in pedestrian-hostile buildings and large roadways are difficult to change and will be in place for generations to come.

Terminal cities can be somewhat improved with a Transformation Strategy.

Preventing City Degradation

Implementation rules prevent developers, architects, transportation engineers, and others from degrading a city.

A developer's primary motive is profit. If the community's values regarding the relationship of a building to the street are not well-defined, it is likely that those concerns will not be part of a developer's priorities. If the defining approach is "let the market decide," the city has a surefire recipe for creating a pedestrian-hostile environment.

An architect's primary motive is to design and get paid for a building that the client can afford to build. The compatibility of the architectural design with adjacent buildings, or the building's relationship to the street, may not be a top concern. Far too many architects, driven by ego, instinctively want to create a special, one-of-a-kind design statement that stands out and brings accolades. Perhaps the architect will receive an award if the design is truly unique—this will bring business to the architectural firm. The community's values risk being ignored unless design guidelines and standards are in place.

The transportation engineer's primary motive is to move traffic. Increased traffic volumes will quickly make a street pedestrian-hostile—an unfortunate consequence of growth. Attention to the pedestrian and the bicycle rider is generally a lesser priority. When congestion begins to choke the roadways, motorists and politicians want an immediate fix, and the transportation engineer will be the first to hear about it. In the absence of public area standards, downtown streets will inevitably become pedestrian-hostile over time.

Implementation rules are the sole means for making sure the developer, the architect, and the transportation engineer all comply with community values. Without rules in place, cities risk becoming ordinary or terminal.

The Case for Beauty

There are many ways to measure attributes of a city—for example, there are quantifiable standards for livability, education, walkability, transit service, employment, and safety. But a city's beauty is measured in more subtle ways. People are more inclined to value and visit places of beauty—consider Santa Fe, Santa Barbara, Barcelona. It behooves decision-makers to recognize that the effort to create beauty in a city is not frivolous. It is good for business as well as pleasure.

In an effort to define "beauty," it may be helpful to identify the kinds of buildings that detract from a city's attractiveness. They include:

- bunker buildings or buildings with blank walls at the ground floor
- modern buildings inserted into historic districts
- buildings out of scale with their neighbors
- poorly designed buildings with inappropriate materials and details
- parking structures that look like stacked parking lots

Other features that detract from the beauty of a city:

- freeways
- railroad lines

- trash and dirty streets
- garbage containers
- power poles and transmission towers
- overhead wires
- surface parking lots
- billboards, large signage, and advertising of all kinds
- vacant lots
- graffiti
- bad public art
- substandard night lighting

The first step in dealing with these negative features is to recognize that they degrade the city and are not good for business. The next step is to initiate actions to fix the problem or mitigate the impacts.

GUIDELINES AND STANDARDS

City character and livability are determined in large part by what happens at the street level. Consequently, the first priority in developing implementation rules should be the creation of design standards and guidelines that create pedestrian-friendly streets. Sidewalks bordered by blank walls, parking lots, empty forecourts, and driveways create an inhospitable environment and should not be allowed.

Design guidelines are discretionary, not mandatory. Design standards are mandatory.

Design Guidelines

The role of guidelines is to promote appropriate design and construction in a city's central core and neighborhood centers and to discourage the construction of any new building that may have a disruptive effect on the appearance or functionality of the center. These guidelines are applicable to both privately and publicly owned parcels of land. They provide developers and architects with a clear understanding of the city's expectations for new construction. They also provide city officials a framework for reviewing proposed projects. Guidelines encourage everyone to play by the same rules.

At a very minimum, design guidelines should provide information on:

- community character, including unique historical features or other special architectural attributes that must be respected
- pedestrian needs, including techniques for creating pedestrian-friendly streets and spaces
- architectural requirements, including characteristics that maintain high-quality, compatible development
- lighting, including concepts for illuminating buildings and streets to improve business opportunities and security
- signs, including functional and tasteful ways to identify commercial services and/or building tenants

Guidelines need to illustrate both what is acceptable and what is not. For example, contemporary buildings inserted into a historic district can erode the visual integrity of the district when they are not visually compatible with adjacent historic structures and should be deemed unacceptable. Cities should be very clear about what is not acceptable in order to prevent unacceptable design solutions from being submitted for approval.

Compatible Historic/
Contemporary Buildings

Incompatible Historic/
Contemporary Buildings

Incompatible building design can have a significant impact on a city when a large number of incompatible buildings create visual chaos. The consequences will lead to the creation of a city center that is not attractive to the public or the investor.

Cities that have unified design themes are cities that people like to visit. Santa Fe is a good example. Its design guidelines stipulate that only buildings in the Pueblo or Territorial Style will be approved. Unlike Santa Fe, however, many communities do not have design guidelines in place that prevent contemporary buildings from being insensitively inserted into the historic fabric of the city. Even a single out-of-character building is hard to tolerate—but a number of such buildings can significantly erode a downtown's unique visual character. Eventually, a downtown can lose its distinctiveness altogether, becoming a place people no longer want to visit or invest.

Design guidelines are needed to keep architects from degrading cities. It is not uncommon for building owners or public agencies to ask for assistance in reigning-in architects who are set on selling designs that are inappropriate. A classic example was the proposed design for a forty-room guesthouse for conference attendees at the Johnson Foundation's international educational facility in Racine, Wisconsin— a campus which includes the famous Frank Lloyd Wright house, Wingspread. Completed in 1939, Wingspread, a National Historic Landmark, is the last and largest of Wright's prairie-style homes. The proposed guesthouse would have been twice the size of Wingspread. I was asked to intervene.

Sam Johnson and the Foundation President, Boyd Gibbons, asked me to review a preliminary site plan and design for the proposed building. The design had two major flaws. First, the proposed guesthouse was sited too close to Wingspread; its large size would have diminished Wingspread's prominence, relegating it to the role of a secondary structure. Second, the overall design for the guesthouse was a caricature of Wingspread rather than a sensitive homage to Wright's majestic house. The Foundation didn't want to mimic its famous landmark building, but it did want to have a respectful neighbor.

The Foundation decided to hire a new architect for the project— a talented Wisconsin firm who assured the Foundation that their building would be compatible with Wingspread. I was retained to represent the Foundation and provide design oversight. When the preliminary concepts for the revised guesthouse were submitted for review, I was shocked. The design by the newly hired architects was completely unrelated to the character and quality of Wright's famous building. It was a tight-skinned, super slick, contemporary design that screamed out "look at me." I rejected the design and gave the design team a summary of Wright's design fundamentals for their edification.

A new designer from the Wisconsin firm was assigned to the project. Using Wright's design vocabulary, he produced an acceptable design for the guesthouse—one that was horizontal in character with large overhangs. The new guesthouse, which sits comfortably on the site, is a good neighbor and plays a secondary role to Wingspread.

The design of a carousel museum in Albany, Oregon, provides

another example of the challenges in designing a building that fits into a pre-existing context. In this case, a talented Oregon architect had been retained to design a building that was to house a carousel carved by a group of Albany artists and craftsmen. Albany has a wonderful stock of historic downtown buildings, and the carousel museum had been designated the anchor building at the end of the town's historic Main Street. I was retained by the city as its design consultant.

The architect clearly understood the parameters of the project before accepting the job. Even so, in the first meeting with the client, he showed up with three design alternatives, all with a slick contemporary character. The client, needless to say, was not happy. After weeks of wrangling, the architect resigned the commission.

A more recent example of these kinds of compatibility challenges is the new City Hall in downtown Whitefish, Montana. Whitefish is a popular destination for tourists who ski in the winter or tour Glacier National Park in the summer. Its downtown is filled with many historic buildings.

A Montana architectural firm was selected after assuring city officials that their design for City Hall would be compatible with the historic downtown. Unfortunately, their preliminary design was more contemporary than historical, and the city was not pleased. After many unproductive negotiations with the architects, I was asked to provide design oversight on behalf of the city's interests.

Whitefish officials understood that inserting a contemporary building into the downtown would erode its historic character and, in turn, the economy and investment environment. Ultimately, a final design was approved, after the architects removed trendy contemporary features that were foreign to the town's character.

I have had many similar experiences with other architects who were not responsive to the pre-existing urban environment. It is essential for a city to take the initiative and adopt design guidelines and design review procedures that keep future construction from degrading its unique cityscape.

Design Guidelines Checklist

Design guidelines contain both written descriptions and photographs of acceptable and unacceptable building designs. Not every guideline may apply to a particular project.

A one-page checklist is a helpful tool for summarizing the guidelines for a proposed project and for determining whether or not a project is in compliance.

DESIGN GUIDELINES CHECKLIST

Project and Applicant Name: _____

Zoning: _____

Building Use: _____

Other: _____

Submission Date: _____

DESIGN GUIDELINES

	Applies		Complies	
	Yes	No	Yes	No
1). Character				
• Establish a Northern Cities Design Vernacular	☐	☐	☐	☐
• Reuse Historic Buildings	☐	☐	☐	☐
• Consider the Climate	☐	☐	☐	☐
• Integrate Art	☐	☐	☐	☐
2). Pedestrian Emphasis				
• Reinforce the Pedestrian System	☐	☐	☐	☐
• Create Successful Outdoor Spaces	☐	☐	☐	☐
• Integrate Accessible Design	☐	☐	☐	☐
3). Architecture				
• Promote Architectural Compatibility	☐	☐	☐	☐
• Foster Vertical Rhythm and Massing	☐	☐	☐	☐
• Promote Varied Roof Forms	☐	☐	☐	☐
• Build Compatible Parking Structures	☐	☐	☐	☐
• Use Quality Wall Materials	☐	☐	☐	☐
• Promote Historic Window Forms	☐	☐	☐	☐
• Integrate Arcades	☐	☐	☐	☐
• Protect the Pedestrian from the Elements	☐	☐	☐	☐
• Provide Inviting Doors	☐	☐	☐	☐
• Promote Welcoming Residential Doors	☐	☐	☐	☐
• Encourage Corner Entries	☐	☐	☐	☐
• Encourage Inviting Ground-Floor Windows	☐	☐	☐	☐
• Create a Rich Building Edge	☐	☐	☐	☐
4). Lighting				
• Promote 'Dark Skies'	☐	☐	☐	☐
• Orient Lighting to the Pedestrian	☐	☐	☐	☐
• Integrate Building Lighting	☐	☐	☐	☐
5). Signs				
• Integrate Wall Signs with Architecture	☐	☐	☐	☐
• Orient Signs to the Pedestrian	☐	☐	☐	☐

Sample Design Guideline Checklist

Building Design Standards

Building design standards ensure that all new development is in compliance with the intent of a Framework Plan. They identify the essential requirements for how a building relates to the public realm (such as sidewalks and streets). For example, design standards may prohibit blank walls at the street level or specify a percentage of wall openings along the sidewalk.

There are many design standards that can improve the downtown pedestrian experience and spur private investment. But none are more important than regulations that:

- require buildings be built up to the sidewalk's edge
- prohibit blank walls
- identify required retail areas

Blank Walls: Not Permitted

Retail: Required

Responsibility for administering design standards can easily be allocated to city staff, because design standards allow no room for interpretation. A project is either in compliance or it is not.

Public Area Standards

Approximately 40% of a downtown's land area is occupied by streets and sidewalks. These constitute the public realm. Public area standards identify design requirements for this realm and for open spaces, such as parks and plazas. Most communities do not have established standards for making the public realm both pedestrian- and bicycle-friendly.

Most transportation engineers are primarily concerned with moving traffic through a city and providing adequate parking for cars. Pedestrians and bicycles can be an afterthought. As traffic volume increases, streets are often widened to accommodate even greater amounts of traffic. Curbside parking is often removed and/or sidewalks narrowed to accommodate more lanes of traffic.

The erosion of the pedestrian environment usually occurs gradually, until the downtown is no longer a friendly place for pedestrians.

Creating public area standards is a necessary step for making the streets pedestrian-friendly once again and for preventing the pedestrian realm from being further degraded.

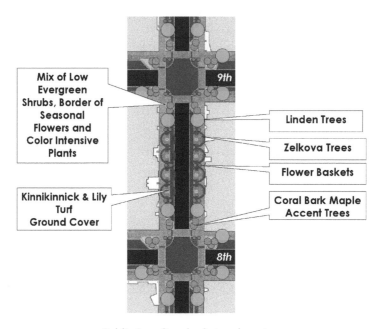

Mix of Low Evergreen Shrubs, Border of Seasonal Flowers and Color Intensive Plants

Linden Trees

Zelkova Trees

Flower Baskets

Kinnikinnick & Lily Turf Ground Cover

Coral Bark Maple Accent Trees

Public Area Standards: Landscaping

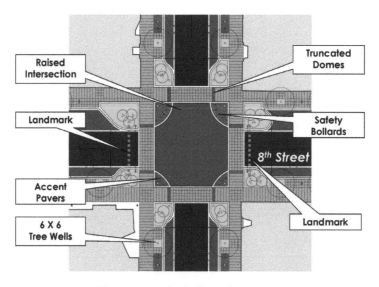

Raised Intersection

Truncated Domes

Landmark

Safety Bollards

Accent Pavers

6 X 6 Tree Wells

Landmark

Public Area Standards: Typical Intersection

Public area standards should address landscaping, lighting and all modes of travel: walking, bicycles, public transit, trucks, and automobiles.

Pedestrian Standards

Pedestrian standards deal with sidewalks, crosswalks, lighting, landscaping, wayfinding, seating, trash receptacles, and newspaper racks.

Bicycle Standards

Bicycle standards include shared-use pathways, separated or protected bicycle lanes, on-street bicycle lanes, bicycle parking, and intersection signals.

Roadway Standards

Roadway standards cover automobile and truck lanes, curbside parking, curb extensions at street corners, curb radii, and transit stops.

Complete Street Standards

Public area standards should also include the design of complete streets in which the pedestrian, the bicycle, public transit, and the automobile are all given consideration, but the pedestrian has the top priority.

The allocation of available space is always the primary concern when trying to increase sidewalk width or add protected bicycle lanes. For example, if sufficient space is not available for protected bike lanes on streets with three or four lanes of traffic, it may be possible to take out a lane of traffic. In many cases, it turns out that a road can function nearly as well with one lane eliminated.

Preparing complete street standards for existing streets can be difficult, and often requires tradeoffs. A typical tradeoff was apparent in the creation of a protected bikeway on both sides of Higgins Avenue in Missoula, Montana—achieved by eliminating a single lane of traffic. In Lincoln, Nebraska, the tradeoff was vacating a lane of traffic in order to provide the space necessary for a bi-directional protected bikeway. Tradeoffs like this are part of a "road diet," because the elimination of a traffic lane slims down the roadway.

In other cases, however, efforts to enhance the pedestrian experience are not as simple as a road diet. For example, in Whitefish, Montana, the task was to make the downtown retail street, Central

Avenue, more pedestrian-friendly. The ten-foot-wide sidewalks were too narrow for a comfortable shopping experience and the intersection pedestrian crossing distances were too wide to feel safe.

The complete street standards we developed for Whitefish included:

- widening the sidewalk by narrowing traffic lanes
- narrowing the distance of pedestrian crossings at the intersections by extending the sidewalks into the parking zone through curb extensions
- eliminating curbs at pedestrian crossings by raising the level of the intersections, so that pedestrians would not have to step off a curb to cross the street

The intent was to prepare complete street standards that would never be dated by fashionable design trends. As a result, all of Whitefish's improvements reflect an elegant simplicity, durability, and timelessness.

DESIGN REVIEW

A design review process is effective only if it is responsive to established design guidelines which reflect the community's values, and

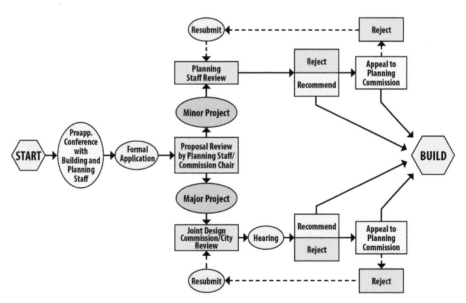

Typical Design Review Process

aspirations for the built environment. The review process can help protect a city's unique identity and attractiveness to private investors.

Design review without design guidelines can be arbitrary and ineffective, yielding biased choices from individuals serving on the design review committee or from members of the public who may be attending the design review sessions. The process can be cumbersome and complicated. The challenge is to make it efficient and effective.

An independent committee not comprised of city planning staff should be established specifically for the purpose of design review. Its directive should be to evaluate all proposed large construction projects relative to their compliance with design guidelines. It is too much to expect city staff to handle the complexities of design review alone—for their jobs might be jeopardized if political pressures arise to approve or reject a particular project.

Not every project needs to be subjected to a formal design review process. Most city administrators have on-staff capacity to review small or minor projects quickly and efficiently.

CHAPTER SIX

Taking Charge

Prepare a Transformation Strategy and success is guaranteed.

I hear the mailbox click in the middle of the night. Going downstairs, I see a plain envelope on the floor. Opening it, I find a check for $100, made out to me, signed by the president of a neighborhood association. There is no note. I am puzzled—our firm had been paid by the city, and the neighborhood association owed us nothing.

The next day I call the association president to ask about the check. He says, "Because we were so grateful that the City Council adopted your recommendations, we thought the least we could do was give you a token gift to express our appreciation. You saved our neighborhood."

The neighborhood had been threatened by a previous plan that would have allowed heavy through-traffic from adjacent suburban development. Had the plan been implemented, traffic volumes on many of their sleepy neighborhood streets would have grown to well over five thousand cars per day. The noise and safety issues associated with those traffic volumes would have seriously degraded the neighborhood.

Using the Transformation Strategy planning process, our firm developed an alternative transportation network that accommodated regional traffic while preventing through-traffic on neighborhood streets. The City Council adopted the strategy recommendations unanimously.

Such situations are not atypical of what our firm finds in many cities. In most cases it isn't that the city hasn't planned. They have. But, their plans are seriously flawed—like the proposed transportation plan in this story. The concept was what we call a silver bullet—a well-intentioned plan that on the surface appears attractive but would actually harm the city. Or, more commonly, we find a plan that is so general that most anything is permitted, resulting in the city's degradation over time.

We tell cities that success is guaranteed if they prepare a Transformation Strategy: problems are solved, new investment created, and the quality of life improved. Success is largely due to (1) a systematic planning process, (2) an emphasis on preparing and evaluating detailed urban design alternatives, (3) meaningful public involvement, and (4) a realistic implementation strategy.

The business of transforming cities is a demanding pursuit. But the satisfaction of knowing that you have made a difference is tremendously rewarding. The spontaneous expressions of appreciation that happen during a project—like a heartfelt thank-you that comes through the mailbox in the middle of the night—make all the hard work worthwhile.

INITIATING A TRANSFORMATION STRATEGY

Once a city has decided that it wants to prepare a Transformation Strategy, the following steps should be followed to ensure that it will be successful.

Identify the Need

The first step in undertaking a Transformation Strategy is to develop an agreement about the objectives of the strategy. Typically, city staff and elected officials, in cooperation with public activists, develop the objectives.

Establish a Budget

A Framework Plan and public support for a small city can cost up to $400,000. The amount for a larger city may range $500,000 to $2,000,000. The cost for developing implementation rules is additional.

Prepare a Request for Proposals (RFP)

City staff members are responsible for preparing a Request for Proposals (RFP). An RFP typically includes a list of the issues to be addressed; an outline of the work to be performed; a timeline; the process that will be used for selecting a consultant team; and specifications regarding the documentation consultants are required to provide in order to be considered for the job—such as resumes, staff organizational structure, prior experience with similar projects, and so forth.

A budget should always be included in the RFP. Some cities prefer to ask consultants how much they will charge for services rendered. This approach is ill-advised because of the temptation to give the work to the lowest bidder, not the most qualified team. Knowing that the lowest fee will probably determine who gets the job, skilled professionals may ignore the project altogether.

Obtain Approvals

Before an RFP is released, key decision-makers in the city administration need to approve the proposed project. Decision-makers usually want to see a statement of need, the proposed budget, and a copy of the RFP.

Release the RFP

RFPs can be published on various national websites used by the planning profession. Both the American Planning Association (APA) and Planetizen maintain well-respected websites that list active RFPs nationwide.

It can cost a consultant as much as $5,000/$20,000 to prepare a response to an RFP. If twenty consultants respond, the total cost to the consultant community may approach $400,000. To mitigate these costs, some cities restrict responses to a select, by-invitation-only group of five to ten qualified firms.

Select the Best Consultant

A small group—ideally consisting of a mix of city staff, business leaders, and public activists—should be assembled to review the responses to the RFP. They will select three to five top consultants, conduct interviews, and evaluate the teams. Generally, ninety minutes or less is sufficient time for an interview, with approximately thirty minutes of that time allocated to the consultant's presentation and the remainder to questions and answers.

Evaluation criteria for selecting a professional planning firm to prepare a Transformation Strategy should include (1) strong design capability, (2) the number of Transformation Strategies or similar work completed to date, along with (3) examples and analysis of the relative success of the firm's plans, and (4) previous, if any, work with retail transformation strategies. This is a critical factor, because generating retail activity is often the primary and most challenging part of a transformation effort. Without considerable experience in the retail sector, a consultant team will be seriously handicapped.

Scoring criteria should be provided to the potential candidate prior to interviews. All members of the selection committee should fill out scoring sheets.

MANAGING A TRANSFORMATION STRATEGY

Responsibilities

A city governmental agency such as a Planning Bureau serves as the client for a Transformation Strategy. It is responsible for hiring the lead consultant, administering the contract, and identifying a staff person to manage the project. The agency also provides the consultant team with relevant background materials, reviews documents and products produced by the consultant, and schedules meetings with the public and local interest groups.

A steering committee should be convened to provide additional oversight. Members of the steering committee should be key figures in the life of the city, such as public officials and business and civic leaders. The job of the steering committee is to review the progress of the work during each phase of the study and at completion. It is important that the committee be large enough to represent diverse community interests. It is not unusual to have fifteen to thirty people on a steering committee.

Lead Consultant

Typically, the lead consultant is responsible for coordinating the efforts of any subconsultants who may be required. For example, there may be a need for a subconsultant with expertise in transportation or market economics. Sometimes unique conditions in the study area require in-depth knowledge that only a subconsultant can provide.

The lead consultant should also be responsible for managing and conducting the public involvement program. This approach is preferable to hiring a public relations or public-engagement sub-contractor—for the public should have direct contact with the lead consultants, hearing their ideas and rationales for the alternatives they are proposing. Hearing proposals from a public-involvement facilitator disconnects city residents from the experts whose job it is to create appropriate solutions for transforming their city.

Subconsultants

Subconsultants work for and are managed by the lead consultant. The role of a transportation subconsultant, for example, is to identify circulation issues and to propose solutions. A successful Transformation Strategy requires a transportation consultant who understands that the highest priorities are pedestrians, transit, and bicycles, rather than automobiles. The subconsultant must be willing to push back against city and state highway engineers who may hold a strong bias towards automobile-based solutions. Unfortunately, transportation consultants with these strengths and values are not easy to find.

In a typical planning study, the task of the market subconsultant is to make economic projections about future market demands for new development by looking at established growth trends. In the preparation of a Transformation Strategy, the market subconsultant performs two additional tasks. First, the subconsultant evaluates the development potential of each land-use and transportation alternative. The subconsultant also estimates the public revenue that can be expected from each of the proposed solutions.

Public Support

A Transformation Strategy will not be implemented unless it has widespread public support. Public support is achieved through public and stakeholder meetings that are held throughout the planning process. Ideally, one large public meeting lasting between two to three hours will be held during each of the four or five phases. Additionally, numerous stakeholder and interest group meetings of not more than an hour in length should be convened during each phase, to solicit the thinking of these individuals and to keep them informed as the strategy is developed. It is not unusual to have between ten and twenty stakeholder meetings during each phase. To facilitate public understanding of the issues, consultants should present proposed solutions in a clear, simple, three-dimensional format as it can be difficult for non-professionals to interpret planning diagrams. At all times, the proposed land-use and transportation alternatives should be explained with reference to the specific problems identified at the onset of the study.

Throughout the duration of the project, it is valuable to brief key decision-makers and public officials so that they are familiar with the work, and to obtain their comments and suggestions. Key city officials who are fully informed and assured that their ideas and concerns are addressed are far more likely to be advocates of a completed Transformation Strategy.

Cities that have been most successful in developing and implementing plans are those that actively engage the general public and civic organizations in the process. Though the lone voice can be helpful, decision-makers generally pay more attention to people who represent respected local organizations with active and committed memberships.

Civic organizations that have been effective in promoting change in cities where I have worked include:

- retail associations
- neighborhood associations

- culture and tourism associations
- the League of Women Voters
- climate action coalitions
- advocates for affordable and homeless housing
- economic development task forces
- the Chamber of Commerce

Individuals and representatives from civic organizations can participate in the planning process by:

- attending public meetings and advocating for needed change
- reviewing draft planning documents and suggesting improvements
- serving on planning commissions
- serving as an elected official

These organizations can promote progressive planning practices by:

- advocating for a Transformation Strategy
- working to elect progressive leadership
- discouraging piecemeal planning
- promoting the hiring of qualified city planning staff
- opposing silver bullet projects

Implementing the Transformation Strategy

Adopt the Strategy

The first step in the implementation of a Transformation Strategy is formal adoption by the city administration. Without that, the strategy will have no legal status, and potential investors and the community will not take the study's recommendations seriously.

Implement the Strategy

The first five years following the adoption of a Transformation Strategy are the most critical. While the implementation of recommended projects and programs may continue for up to ten years, if significant action isn't taken and progress made within the first five, the strategy will become a shelf plan.

A committee that includes community decision-makers and representatives from public interest groups should be appointed to oversee implementation. The committee's responsibility is to assure that the recommendations of the implementation strategy are fulfilled. The implementation committee should prepare annual reports for the mayor and City Council that summarize the accomplishments of the past year, and identify implementation objectives for the coming year.

An implementation committee is necessary if a city is serious about creating early implementation momentum and keeping the strategy from becoming another shelf plan.

Update the Strategy

A Transformation Strategy should be updated every five to ten years in response to new issues and changing conditions. The city administration and the political establishment can change dramatically over a period of five years, and with change comes the loss of institutional memory. While city staff and elected officials come and go, the implementation committee should remain in place—and, when necessary, act to initiate an update to the strategy.

CHAPTER SEVEN

Radical Transformation Strategy

There is no escaping climate change.

We are one interconnected world and climate change will affect all people in all places. How we deal with the consequences of our collective neglect is the preeminent moral challenge of our time.

My firm has developed city plans for over twenty years. During that time, climate change has become a critical concern. Unfortunately, during that same period transportation carbon emissions from cars and trucks have increased. Clearly, traditional public planning processes have not provided cities with the information they need to reverse this destructive trend.

Portland's recent planning activities are illustrative. The city's population is expected to increase from 620,000 to 880,000 by 2035—a 42% gain—and congestion is already plaguing the metropolitan area. After several years of intensive planning, Portland recently completed the 2035 Comprehensive Plan and will soon complete the 2035 Central City Plan. Both lack convincing strategies for addressing Portland's most critical issues: accommodating growth, reducing congestion, and addressing climate change.

What has gone wrong? We need urban design solutions that are responsive to a changing world.

Public servants who work in urban agencies are not charged with providing the radical rethinking needed to produce visionary land use and transportation plans that adequately respond to a warming climate.

Where does Portland go from here? After years of unfruitful effort, the city is not in a position to initiate yet another planning process. However, there is an immediate need to identify what Portland—and indeed all cities—must do to reduce carbon emissions. The Radical Transformation Strategy described in this chapter provides an approach that can address this critical issue.

Private foundations would fund the process. Consultants with the technical expertise needed to develop creative solutions would perform the work. Public agency involvement would be limited to positions on advisory committees. At a later date, if Portland wanted to implement all or part of the Radical Transformation Strategy, an extensive public participation program would be required to educate the public, refine the strategy, and build public support for implementation.

The Portland Radical Transformation Strategy is supported by Portland climate activists and has been endorsed by Portland's mayor Ted Wheeler.

The Radical Transformation Strategy is not limited to Portland—other cities may adapt the strategy to identify solutions too complex to consider in a typical Transformation Strategy.

Implementation
Costs, Financing, and Phasing

Design Framework
Integrated Land Use/Transportation Plan

Goals
Desired Outcomes

Radical Transformation Strategy Basic Elements

AN INVESTIGATIVE PROCESS

A Radical Transformation Strategy is developed through a design and research process. It provides answers to issues related to climate change. For example, goals might be to:

- reduce vehicle miles traveled by 50%
- reduce carbon emissions by 80%
- reduce auto congestion without building new roads or expanding existing roadways
- transition urban and suburban areas from auto dependency to bike, pedestrian, and transit friendly neighborhoods
- accommodate population growth resulting from an influx of climate refugees leaving areas being impacted by climate extremes

A Radical Transformation Strategy is:

- prepared by consultants
- funded by private foundations
- managed and reviewed with the assistance of a public Policy Advisory Committee (PAC) and a Technical Advisory Committee (TAC)

In contrast, a Transformation Strategy is developed through a public process. Public agencies manage the process and the public is involved throughout. This process provides solutions to issues that are of immediate concern to the public and decision-makers. Typical objectives might be to:

- enhance existing downtown retail
- locate and design a public plaza
- provide more parking
- provide affordable housing
- preserve historic buildings
- plant more street trees

A Transformation Strategy is:

- prepared by a public agency
- funded with public money
- developed with participation from an educated public

Like a Transformation Strategy, the Radical Transformation Strategy has three basic parts and will not be successful if any one of the three is missing.

Part One: Goals

Desired outcomes related to congestion, growth, and climate change will be established. A fundamental goal is to shorten and eliminate auto trips.

Part Two: Design Framework

Existing employment and neighborhood centers will be evaluated for their neighborhood district MOD and BOD potential. Locations for additional neighborhood districts will be determined. Site-specific urban designs will be prepared for neighborhood districts to ensure that they can accommodate (1) a significant amount of additional market rate and affordable housing and (2) the mix of uses required in a vibrant commercial hub. Commercial hubs in neighborhood districts will be connected to protected bikeway and transit networks. Benefits of the integrated land use/transportation plans will be quantified.

Part Three: Implementation

Projects with the potential to significantly reduce carbon emissions will be identified. Site-specific congestion pricing alternatives will be tested. Project findings (costs, financing, and phasing recommendations) will be developed and summarized in written reports and video formats.

PORTLAND ISSUES

Accommodating future growth, reducing auto congestion, and significantly reducing greenhouse gas emissions are fundamental planning issues for Portland. Left unaddressed, they will create conditions that have the potential to seriously degrade Portland's quality of life.

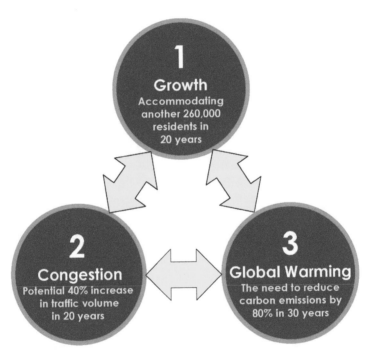

Fundamental Portland Planning Issues

Growth

Portland's population of 620,000 is projected to increase by 260,000—42% in twenty years. However, climate change may double that number.

Portland's 2035 Comprehensive Plan is vague about how the original projection will be accommodated—much less the greater number.

Currently, the City of Portland assumes that growth can be accommodated (1) along major transportation corridors, and (2) in retail/employment centers. However, the suitability of dense housing development along corridors with heavy traffic volumes is questionable. This strategy is in direct conflict with the need to create pedestrian-friendly neighborhoods.

In addition, since detailed plans for centers have not been developed, there is no way to assess their viability.

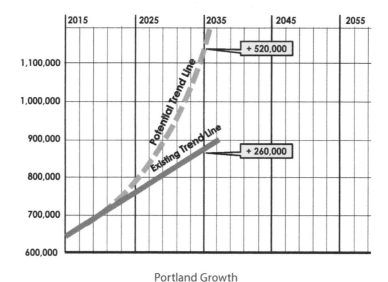

Portland Growth

Congestion

According to a 2015 annual report by the Texas A&M Transportation Institute, Portland is the twelfth most congested city in the country—tied with Atlanta, Austin, and Miami. And according to a study released at the 2015 Oregon Business Summit, congestion is expected to get exponentially worse. The study indicated that the average metropolitan household will be stuck in congestion sixty-nine hours per year by 2040—triple the time spent in 2010. Compounding the problem, Portland-area freeways are now operating at or above capacity. Portland residents do not need statistics to prove that congestion is a problem. Everyone has stories about being late for work, meetings, and social events because of severe congestion.

Portland Congestion

Climate Change

Experts predict that if greenhouse gas emissions keep increasing, many southern cities could experience temperatures exceeding 100 degrees Fahrenheit for extended periods of time. By 2100, even a city as far north as Portland could experience such temperatures for ten to twenty-five days each year.

Despite ambitious legislation passed to cut emissions from the electricity and transportation sectors, Oregon is falling far short. An article in the *Oregonian* (published on February 1, 2017) stated "Oregon is not reducing emissions fast enough to meet its goals for 2020 and beyond. In fact, it's not even close." These were the findings of a biennial report the Oregon Global Warming Commission delivered to state lawmakers. The culprit was identified as "higher emissions from cars, trucks, trains, and buses, as more Oregonians drive more miles and buy less fuel-efficient cars because of population growth, a strong economy, and cheap gas."

Since 62% of Oregon's population resides within the Portland Metropolitan Area, Portland's efforts are critical if the state is going to meet its greenhouse gas emission goals.

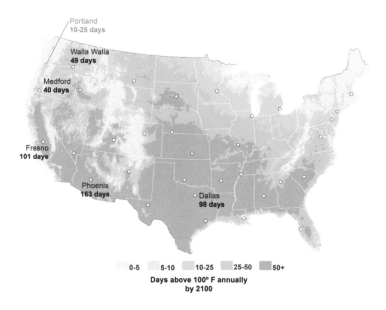

Source: Think It's Hot Now? Graphics by Tim Wallace and Bill Marsh. Accessed 28 March 2018.
https://www.nytimes.com/interactive/2016/08/20/sunday-review/climate-change-hot-future.html

Other Portland Planning Issues

The primary challenge for the Portland Radical Transformation Strategy will be to develop a Design Framework responsive to growth, congestion, and climate change. Development of the Design Framework is fundamental and will allow other important social and structural issues to be addressed:

- affordable housing
- homelessness
- jobs
- education
- quality of life
- recreation
- environmental health
- gentrification

For example, the Design Framework will identify specific sites for affordable housing, jobs, and education facilities.

PORTLAND RADICAL TRANSFORMATION STRATEGY

The proposed Portland Radical Transformation Strategy provides a compelling vision of what Portland must do to become proactive in regard to climate issues.

Neighborhood districts (BODs and MODs) are fundamental building blocks for development of the Portland Radical Transformation Strategy. Other fundamental building blocks include:

- Networks of High Capacity Transit (HCT), in exclusive right-of-way lanes, linked to neighborhood district commercial hubs and trip generators such as job centers.

- Networks of protected bikeways connected to neighborhood district commercial hubs and trip generators.

- Congestion pricing options for local and regional road networks.

Common congestion pricing options include:

- **Variably priced lanes**, involving variable tolls on separated lanes within a highway, such as Express Toll Lanes or High Occupancy Toll lanes

- **Variable tolls** on entire roadways – both on toll roads and bridges, as well as on existing toll-free facilities during rush hours

- **Cordon charges** – either variable or fixed charges to drive within or into a congested area within a city

- **Area-wide charges** – per-mile charges on all roads within an area

FUNDAMENTAL BUILDING BLOCKS

BOD

MOD

Protected Bikeways

Streetcar

Bus Rapid Transit

Light Rail

Potential Energy Savings

Portland now uses Center and TOD planning models with a radius of a quarter to a half a mile. Transportation energy savings for Centers and TODs are estimated to be 6–11%. In contrast, transportation energy savings for the BOD and MOD, with their larger one-mile radius, are estimated to be 27–51%.

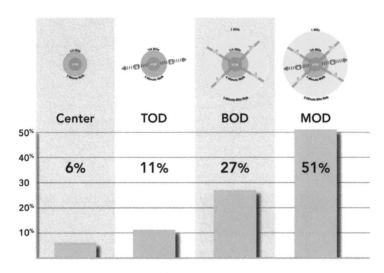

Transportation Energy Savings

Initiating Work

The following description of the steps needed to initiate the Portland Radical Transformation Strategy, is illustrative of an approach many other cities might take. The steps, in sequence, include:

- preparing a detailed Radical Transformation Strategy work program
- identifying project sponsors & endorsers
- preparing funding proposals
- obtaining funding
- finalizing the management structure
- retaining advisory committees
- identifying and retaining the consultant team
- starting work

Products

Three products would be produced:

1. *Portland Radical Transformation Strategy*—a user-friendly document that illustrates what Portland must do to accommodate growth, reduce congestion, and reduce carbon emissions significantly.

2. *City Transformation Strategy*—Findings and recommendations from the *Portland Radical Transformation Strategy* will be used to develop a document illustrating universal transformation concepts that apply to cities everywhere.

3. *Radical Transformation Strategy Educational Materials*—Website, video, and handouts will be developed to educate decision makers and the public about:
   - the need for a Radical Transformation Strategy
   - the benefits associated with a Radical Transformation Strategy
   - how to develop a Radical Transformation Strategy

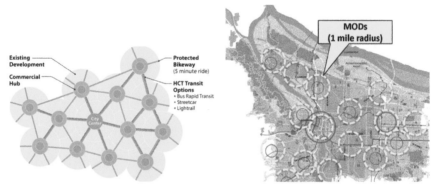

Neighborhood Districts Applied to a City

Neighborhood Districts Applied to Portland

Funding

The process of funding the Portland Radical Transformation Strategy would be similar to the process used to fund two previous Portland area studies that provided critical information to decision makers. The first, *A New Approach to Regional Planning (RAPP)* was sponsored by the Architecture Foundation of Oregon (AFO). The second, *The Land Use, Transportation, Air Quality Project (LUTRAQ)* was sponsored by 1000 Friends of Oregon. Both were funded by local and national foundations. The budget for LUTRAQ was $1.9 million.

Team

Local and national experts who have demonstrated cutting-edge thinking about transformation issues would develop the strategy. The team would include a number of different disciplines, including:

- urban design
- transportation engineering
- energy analysis
- graphic simulation
- economic analysis
- communications

Two local advisory committees would be responsible for reviewing project progress and recommendations. The first would be a Policy Advisory Committee (PAC). Membership should include local and regional decision-makers. The second would be a local Technical Advisory Committee (TAC). Membership would include agency managers and agency technical experts.

Draft Work Program

The Portland Radical Transformation Strategy could be completed in twenty-four months.

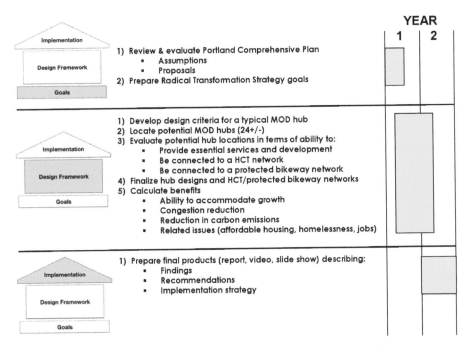

Radical Transformation Strategy Work Program and Schedule

THE FUTURE

Climate change is a threat to all people all over the earth. Unfortunately planning models that show how to retrofit a city in response to this global threat do not exist. My hope is that cities will use the transportation and land use models I have proposed to dramatically reduce carbon emissions and at the same improve the quality of life for all citizens.

POSTSCRIPT

A Call for a New Profession

Most books written about urban design and planning have a narrow focus or are based on abstract theory. This book is different. It is based on my broad range of experience as an architect and urban designer who has transformed cities.

When our urban design firm, Crandall Arambula, was established in 1998, it became obvious that we needed to develop a planning process that *guaranteed* success if we were to get repeat business and recommendations from our clients. We call that process the Transformation Strategy. It has been refined over time as we identify what works and what doesn't.

Architects are rarely aware of contextual issues in cities—land use, circulation, and quality of life. This is not surprising. Architects are trained to design stand-alone buildings. Furthermore, their clients often dictate inappropriate design requirements that architects are obligated to follow. In cities everywhere, the result is a degraded urban environment, hostile to pedestrians.

Planners often create other problems for cities. They are familiar with contextual issues and understand the need for public involvement, but have little design training. The design component of plans is often weak or missing. In the absence of a design framework and specific design proposals, effective implementation strategies can't be developed. Planning documents that are full of words and little else do not get implemented.

If architects tend to degrade cities and planners produce ineffective plans, what needs to change? I recommend the creation of a new profession. The educational curriculum would feature both the design emphasis found in architectural schools and the emphasis on context and public involvement found in planning schools.

The challenge is for the American Institute of Architects (AIA) and the American Planning Association (APA) to work with educators to create a hybrid curriculum. The objective would be to train a new breed of professionals who would create strategies to (1) improve the quality of life in cities and (2) address climate change, as it is imperative for cities to significantly reduce carbon emissions. These new professionals might be called Urban Architects.

Acknowledgments

Don Arambula and I founded Crandall Arambula twenty years ago. His urban design excellence and values are reflected in the innovative concepts in *Fixing Your City*.

Thanks to Carol Raphael, the developmental editor, for asking all the hard questions.

Thanks to Jessie Maran, who suggested many improvements to the final draft of the manuscript.

I would be remiss in not thanking the many planning staffs, civic leaders and concerned citizens in cities where I have worked for their selfless commitment to community service.

And finally, Marilyn Sewell, my wife and confidant, minister, writer, and theologian was the inspiration for my writing the book. Her editing throughout the process was necessary and very much appreciated.

About the Author

GEORGE CRANDALL, FAIA has been responsible for more than 50 key urban design projects across the United States and in Canada. He has helped make Portland a model for planning in America.

Crandall has been involved in the life of cities as an architect and urban designer, as well as a passionate and dedicated citizen activist for over 40 years. In 1998 he founded the consulting firm Crandall Arambula, which specializes in working with cities of all sizes that seek urban transformation. The firm's work has received numerous awards for innovative and effective solutions to seemingly intractable problems.

Because of his extensive experience designing retail, commercial, housing, and transportation projects, he has acquired a unique set of insights and skills. His urban designs attract major private investment, address climate change, and improve quality of life for citizens.

Throughout his career he has been active in numerous professional and civic organizations. He served as President of the Architectural Foundation of Oregon, Board President for 1000 Friends of Oregon, President of the Portland Chapter of the American Institute of Architects (AIA), Chair of the Portland AIA Urban Design Committee, and Chair of the Oregon Governor's Energy Conservation Board.

He has a Bachelor of Architecture and a Bachelor of Science degree in civil engineering from the University of Arizona.

CPSIA information can be obtained
at www.ICGtesting.com
Printed in the USA
BVHW021409120522
636888BV00017B/305